Teacher Education
for Social Justice:
Perspectives and Lessons Learned

Teacher Education
for Social Justice:
Perspectives and Lessons Learned

Luciana C. de Oliveira
Purdue University

INFORMATION AGE PUBLISHING, INC.
Charlotte, NC • www.infoagepub.com

Library of Congress Cataloging-in-Publication Data

Teacher education for social justice : perspectives and lessons learned /
[edited by] Luciana C. de Oliveira.
    p. cm.
  ISBN 978-1-62396-108-4 (pbk.) – ISBN 978-1-62396-109-1 (hardcover) –
ISBN (invalid) 978-1-62396-110-7 (ebook) 1. Critical pedagogy. 2. Social
justice–Study and teaching. I. De Oliveira, Luciana C., editor of
compilation. II. Miller, Galina. Socially just teaching through the eyes of
Russian immigrants.
  LC196.T38 2013
  370.11'5–dc23
                                    2012042430

DEDICATION

To all of the teachers in my family
and especially my sister,
Ligia Carvalho de Oliveira Mascioli,
whose work with adults was an example of social justice.

A todos os professores da minha familia
e especialmente à minha irmã,
Ligia Carvalho de Oliveira Mascioli,
cujo trabalho com adultos foi um exemplo de justiça social.

CONTENTS

PREFACE

Luciana C. de Oliveira

This volume is intended for an audience of researchers in education and students in advanced undergraduate and graduate courses. It is expected that it will be used in teacher education programs that address social justice work in the preparation of teachers as well as in graduate programs that prepare future faculty to work with teachers.

This book grew out of a seminar taught at Purdue University in the spring semester of 2011 entitled "Teacher Education for Social Justice" and supported by the 2010–2011 Diversity Fellows Program, an initiative of the Purdue University Diversity in the Classroom Project sponsored by the Diversity Resource Office. The purpose of the Diversity Fellows Program is to provide support for faculty development, implementation, and sharing of inclusive approaches to teaching, learning, and assessment in the area of diversity. A group of multiethnic scholars and practitioner researchers explore concepts of teaching for social justice and preparing teachers to work toward social justice in schools and communities. The objectives of this book are to (a) present different perspectives on the preparation of teachers for social justice work, (b) contribute to the existing literature on social justice, and (c) provide pedagogical implications and suggestions

Teacher Education for Social Justice: Perspectives and Lessons Learned, pages ix–x.
Copyright © 2013 by Information Age Publishing

for teacher education programs that want to incorporate social justice into their preparation courses.

I would like to thank the authors in this volume for being amazing graduate students committed to doing social justice work and for contributing to the book. I would also like to thank the Diversity Resource Office at Purdue University for their support for the development of the course. In addition, I thank Steve Athanases for introducing me to research on teacher education through his graduate seminar and for continuing to inspire me with his work in teacher education. I owe a special debt of gratitude to my wonderful administrative assistant, Bonnie Nowakowski, for her outstanding support over the years and especially for collecting all of the forms needed for publication of this book. I am indebted to my editorial assistant, Dave Norris, for his help editing the chapters and careful attention to detail. Thanks also to the production team at Information Age Publishing for making this book possible.

I thank my family for their love and belief in me. Thanks to my mother, Maria do Carmo, for helping and supporting me in every way possible; my brother, Leopoldo, for always being a role model for me since I was a child; and my sister Ligia, to whom this book is dedicated, for her continuing support and dedication to our family. I am grateful to other members of my family for their love and care. I am especially grateful to my husband, Alex Noguera, for his emotional support throughout this project. Thanks for always being there for me when I needed some encouragement.

FOREWORD

Marilyn Cochran-Smith

It is not often that one has the opportunity (and honor) to write the fore-word for a book inspired (at least in part) by her own work. So I was delighted when Luciana de Oliveira invited me to write the Foreword for this book, which is based on the writings of graduate students in her course on teacher education for social justice, a topic to which I am now and have long been deeply committed. Luciana told me that along with many other things, the class read several of the writings I have done on this topic over the years, including my 2004 book, *Walking the Road: Race, Diversity, and Social Justice in Teacher Education,* and my more recent attempts to theorize the idea of teacher education for social justice by interrogating theories of justice, theories of practice, and theories of teacher education/teacher learning (Cochran-Smith, 2010). The goal of the course, as I understand it, was to explore ideas related to teaching for social justice and to consider what it would take to prepare teachers to work for social justice in today's schools and communities. The goal of the multiethnic scholars whose writing is highlighted in this book is to take very seriously what this would mean in their own contexts and situations—in short, to imagine and theorize transformative teacher education.

Teacher Education for Social Justice: Perspectives and Lessons Learned, pages xi–xiv.
Copyright © 2013 by Information Age Publishing
xi

Luciana's invitation prompted me to return to *Walking the Road* and to rethink the ideas I wrote about teacher education then from the vantage point of today's related conflicts and issues. Almost a decade ago, I chose the title of my book based on the phrase from Miles Horton and Paulo Freire's *We Make the Road by Walking: Conversations on Education and Social Change* (1990). Their title, in turn, was derived from poet Antonio Machado's adaptation of the Spanish proverb, "*se hace camino al andar*," which has been translated as, "in walking, the path is made," or "you make the way as you go." Horton and Freire's book was about participatory education as an instrument for social change; it focused on the struggles each of them had had individually in trying to link theory and practice in their lives and in their work toward emancipation. I borrowed and transformed their phrase into "walking the road" as the title for a collection of essays about my own much more modest efforts to put into practice locally and theorize more publicly a commitment to teacher education for social justice. As I wrote then,

> My title is intended to emphasize the journey metaphor—walking, a road that goes on and on, traversing a long route over a long time—a metaphor that is central to what it means to conceptualize and live the notion of teaching and teacher education for social justice. This book makes the case that doing teacher education for social justice is an ongoing, over-the-long-haul kind of process for prospective teachers as well as for teacher educators themselves.

My title is also intended to convey an image of uncertainty—the idea that there is no path already there, you must make the path as you go along, you will never pass over the same path again. This idea is central to understanding both the daily work and the lifetime commitment of teaching and learning to teach for social justice . . . I use "walking the road" to signify the organic link—rather than the dichotomy—between acting and theorizing, practice and scholarship, and between doing teacher education and doing research about teacher education. Here, the words emphasize that in teacher education for social justice, there is an acknowledged and desired dialectical relationship between doing and theorizing.

In rereading my own words, I was prompted to consider where we are now in terms of teaching and teacher education for social justice. Thinking about the contemporary teacher education context and the context of education more broadly, I could not avoid a deep sense of concern and a certain amount of pessimism.

Today, the major discourse in and about teacher education is certainly not about social justice. In fact, although this discourse was never predominant, it has now been substantially marginalized, and neoliberal discourses that emphasize the economy, individualism, and free markets are pervasive. Many scholars have written about the impact on education politics and policies of the ideological shift to neoliberalism, including market-based reforms, high-stakes testing, and other new forms of accountability with dire consequences for failure to meet expectations, consumer choice, charter schools, alternate routes into teaching, competition among schools, and data-driven decision making. As we know, the neoliberal discourse takes a human capital perspective on the link between education and the economy. This is based on the assumption that a nation's place in the knowledge economy depends on the quality of its educational system and that the primary purpose of education is to produce a workforce that can meet the demands of the competitive global market and thus preserve the nation's place in that market. In teacher education, this plays out in a very strong focus on accountability for outcomes, defined in terms of the scores on national and international assessments of the eventual students that teacher candidates will teach. This focus is clearly reflected in the proposed plan of the Obama administration to improve teacher education.

As Apple (2005) argues, neoliberal perspectives have transformed our notion of democracy from a political one into an economic one. Along closely related lines, Kumashiro (2010) has suggested that what has been touted as "the new civil rights movement"—the "no excuses" approach to teaching and teacher education—actually works against the goals historically associated with the Civil Rights movement of the mid-1900s and, in fact, undermines public education by masking the fact that the "new civil rights" actually reinforces stratification of the system and continuation of inequitable opportunities and outcomes. What is perhaps most concerning here is that these new discourses are being stitched into the logic of teacher education so seamlessly that they are already nearly imperceptible, and many people seem to have given in to the conclusion that these perspectives are inevitable.

In the midst of this policy and political context, Luciana de Oliveira's book and the writings of the multiethnic scholars she has brought together in this collection of essays are a breath of fresh air and a sign of hope. In this book, prospective teacher educators take up many provocative issues related to diversity, difference, identity development, privilege, agency, stereotyping, community, language, inequity, advocacy, and transformation; they do so with honesty, intelligence, and courage. De Oliveira organizes the chapters of the book according to the key dimensions of teacher education for social justice: teacher candidate selection and recruitment, pedagogy and curriculum of teacher education programs, the contexts and structures of programs and collaborations, and the outcomes of teacher preparation. The book's rich tapestry is woven out of multiple individual threads of inquiry braided together with several powerful themes. The individual threads include Russian immigrants' perspectives on students' language development and achievement, preparing teachers in the United States and

Japan to meet the needs of immigrant students and multilanguage learners, the need for a transformative teacher education curriculum with new spaces and emphases, teacher education that disrupts dominant discourses regarding Islam, social justice identity development in teacher candidates, teacher education that transforms negative representations of education in Appalachia, small-scale community engagement with Latino/a families and teacher candidates, preparing mathematics teachers to work with culturally and linguistically diverse students and to work for social justice, and the unintended impact of No Child Left Behind on English language learners in a rural school.

Braided together with these multiple and diverse threads are a number of consistent themes. The most important and the strongest of these is the idea that teacher education can be a powerful educational experience—a process intentionally designed to disrupt, transform, rethink, alter, interrogate, and ultimately reinvent deeply ingrained images and assumptions about the ways things are and the ways they might be in schools and classrooms. Each chapter in the book not only makes this argument theoretically but also elaborates how this can be done in the context of the complex challenges posed by particular places and spaces. Taken together, the chapters in the book demonstrate what I referred to earlier as the organic link between doing and theorizing teacher education for social justice. The new teacher educators who have written these chapters will begin their journeys with the goal of transformation and reinvention. This is reason for hope.

REFERENCES

Apple, M. (2005). *Educating the "right" way: Market, standards, God, and inequality.* New York, NY: Routledge.

Cochran-Smith, M. (2004). *Walking the road: Race, diversity, and social justice in teacher education.* New York, NY: Teachers College Press.

Cochran-Smith, M. (2010). Toward a theory of teacher education for social justice. In A. Hargreaves, M. Fullan, D. Hopkins, & A. Lieberman (Eds.), *Second international handbook of educational change* (pp. 445–467). New York, NY: Springer.

Horton, M., & Freire, P. (1990). *We make the road by walking: Conversations on education and social change.* Philadelphia, PA: Temple University Press.

Kumashiro, K. (2010). Seeing the big picture: Troubling movements to end teacher education. *Journal of Teacher Education, 61*(1/2), 56–65.

EDITOR BIOGRAPHY

Luciana C. de Oliveira

Luciana C. de Oliveira is associate professor of Literacy and Language Education and Director of the English Language Learning licensure program in the Department of Curriculum and Instruction at Purdue University. Dr. de Oliveira's research focuses on issues related to teaching English language learners (ELLs) at the K–12 level, including the role of language in learning the content areas of teacher education, advocacy and social justice, and nonnative English-speaking teachers in TESOL. Her book, *Knowing and Writing School History: The Language of Students' Expository Writing and Teachers' Expectations* (2011, Information Age), received the David E. Eskey Award for Curriculum Innovation from California TESOL (CATESOL). She was also the recipient of the Early Career Award conferred by the Bilingual Education Research special interest group of the American Educational Research Association (AERA).

Teacher Education for Social Justice: Perspectives and Lessons Learned, page xv.
Copyright © 2013 by Information Age Publishing

CHAPTER 1

PERSPECTIVES AND LESSONS LEARNED ABOUT TEACHER EDUCATION FOR SOCIAL JUSTICE

Luciana C. de Oliveira

Current developments in education point to the need to address social justice in teacher education programs by focusing on the preparation of teachers with the knowledge, dispositions, and practices to work with culturally and linguistically diverse students as a fundamental responsibility of teacher education (Cochran-Smith, 2004; McDonald, 2005, 2007; Zeichner, 2009). This book extends knowledge in the field by providing multiple perspectives on social justice teacher education and lessons learned after carefully examining current and relevant developments in social justice teacher education.

We continue to have a teaching force of predominantly White, monolingual, English-speaking middle-class females, while students across U.S. public schools are increasingly diverse, coming from various racial, ethnic, and linguistic communities (Chubbuck, 2010; Cochran-Smith, 2010; Cochran-Smith, Barnatt, Lahann, Shakman, & Terrell, 2009). Teachers must be chal-

Teacher Education for Social Justice: Perspectives and Lessons Learned, pages 1–9.
1

lenged to avoid seeing diversity as a deficit (Agarwal, Epstein, Oppenheim, Oyler, & Sonu, 2010), as they support *all* students in academic success. In addition, there continues to be an achievement gap between students of color and low-income students in comparison to their White, middle-class peers. The research base has established that students of color, low-income students, and English language learners (ELLs) need high quality opportunities to learn from teachers who are equipped with the knowledge, skills, and dispositions to improve their educational opportunities and who can see and address structural inequities. In our colleges, we must prepare future faculty to educate such teachers (Darling-Hammond, 2010).

In our graduate programs, we are preparing future faculty who will be teacher educators in a variety of settings and contexts. They will be working with students from diverse backgrounds. Some teacher education programs have a common aim of preparing teachers to recognize, specify, and resist inequity in schools and society (McDonald, 2007), but preparing teachers for such work involves preparing faculty to work in such teacher education programs. Therefore, in our graduate programs, we must focus on social justice and equity as key aspects of a vision of teaching and learning to improve the preparation of teachers to work with students of color, low-income students, and ELLs. This book addresses the published literature by explicitly attending to societal structures and institutionalized oppression that perpetuate inequality. One of the goals of the book is to focus on transformative teacher education that goes beyond a celebratory notion of diversity to a focus on change and action (Banks, 2002), preparing future faculty to prepare teachers who can serve as agents of change, as I have described elsewhere (Athanases & de Oliveira, 2008, 2010; de Oliveira & Athanases, 2007).

This chapter describes the different perspectives and lessons learned that will be the thrust of the book and introduces the main concepts developed. Using Cochran-Smith's (2010) representation of teacher preparation for justice, this chapter maps how the other chapters in the book address the dimensions of (a) recruitment, selection, and retention of teacher candidates; (b) curriculum and pedagogy; (c) contexts, structures, and collaborators; and (d) outcomes. The purpose, significance, scope, and organization of the book are introduced.

APPLYING A THEORY OF TEACHER PREPARATION FOR JUSTICE

Many teacher education programs stress social justice, equity, and diversity as essential concerns in teacher education. As we prepare new teacher educators and researchers, they must know what work has been done to prepare teachers to work with culturally and linguistically diverse students, an increasing population in our classrooms. Cochran-Smith (2010) conceptualizes a theory of teacher education for social justice by addressing three main domains: a theory of justice, a theory of practice, and a theory of teacher preparation. In this chapter, I use her third domain, a theory of teacher preparation, in which she elaborates on how teachers learn to teach for justice and the structures that enable such learning in order to describe how the different chapters address this important aspect of teacher education for social justice.

Four key dimensions are identified by Cochran-Smith (2010) as integral to conceptualizing teacher preparation for justice: (a) who should teach, related to the recruitment, selection, and retention of teacher candidates; (b) what teachers and students should learn, or the curriculum and pedagogy of teacher education programs; (c) how and from/with whom teachers learn, related to the contexts, structures, and collaborators; and (d) how these aspects are assessed, or the outcomes of teacher preparation. She further highlights that teacher preparation for social justice is transformative and collaborative and includes working within and against the accountability system. Using these four dimensions as a way to organize the book, a summary of the chapters is presented next.

Recruitment, Selection, and Retention of Teacher Candidates

This dimension has to do with the diversification of the teaching force in terms of cultural, racial, and linguistic backgrounds and the recruitment of teachers who hold beliefs and values consistent with the objectives of social justice (Cochran-Smith, 2010). The chapters that address this dimension include a focus on the recruitment and retention of minority teachers and the importance of diversifying the teaching force to provide role models for all students.

In Chapter 2, "Socially Just Teaching Through the Eyes of Russian Immigrants," Galina Miller and Lyubov Sylayeva use their personal experiences as means to critically reflect on the notion of social justice and explore socially just teaching through the second-language acquisition lens and empowerment framework. Furthermore, being immigrants themselves, they find it significant to ascertain the importance of understanding one's identity construction and its negotiations in order to facilitate the educational achievements of *all* students toward the goal of becoming active citizens. Their reflections address the importance of diversifying the teaching force in terms of cultural, racial, and linguistic backgrounds. Their beliefs, experiences, and values are consistent with social justice goals. They recognize that enacting socially just teaching is an ongoing process and believe that the incorporation of culturally and linguistically responsive pedagogical practices, a devoted commitment to social justice, and English language learning (ELL) education can contribute toward the elimination of achievement disproportions, the power afforded by privilege, and inequitable hierarchies.

Chapter 3, "Teacher Education for Immigrant Students: The Educational Issues of Immigrant Students in the United States and Japan," by Thu Ya Aung, Shaivi Divatia, and Reiko Akiyama, discusses the elements that are needed in teacher education programs to help better serve immigrant children by discussing prominent issues in both the United States and Japan. They describe the need to prepare White teachers for an increasing population of immigrant students in the United States and to prepare Japanese teachers for an increasing population of immigrant students in Japan. In addition to addressing teacher preparation at the preservice and in-service levels, recruitment, and retention of teachers are also addressed. Aung, Divatia, and Akiyama discuss the importance of hiring multicultural teachers to help immigrant children settle in their new environment and acquire a sense of belonging to the community. They conclude with suggestions to address ongoing issues in both the United States and Japan.

Curriculum and Pedagogy

This dimension focuses on curriculum and pedagogy that foster justice and encompass opportunities for teacher candidates "to learn about subject matter, pedagogy, culture, language, the social and cultural contexts of schooling, and the purposes of education" (Cochran-Smith, 2010, p. 459). The chapters that address this dimension provide ideas for inclusion of different aspects of social justice as a focus of curriculum and pedagogy in various contexts.

In Chapter 4, "Chocolate-Covered Twinkies: Social Justice and Superficial Aims in Teacher Education," Jubin Rahatzad, Jason Ware, and Mark Haugen propose an alternate socially transformative vision grounded in Freireian pedagogy for teacher education programs. Such a pedagogy presupposes that human beings' main vocation is to act upon and transform their world, understanding the interrelationships of power, politics, culture, and history within the educational process. They describe the need for *conscientização* to negotiate the demands of dominant culture while cultivating space for agency to impact knowledge construction and value systems (Freire, 2000). The chapter addresses the curriculum changes needed in teacher education in order to reach K–12 students, preservice teachers, and teacher educators and propose (a) a university campus space within local public schools; (b) required second-language proficiency and an immersive study-abroad experience; (c) critical engagement of educational policy, working tensions between the current social order and alternate visions, and; (d) admissions procedures to holistically assess prospective teachers. Aspects of this alternative vision are interconnected and can potentially have an impact on teacher education.

Chapter 5, "Beyond Dominant Discourse on Islam: Proposal for Disruptions Through Teacher Education Programs for Democratic Engagement and Social Justice," also addresses curriculum and pedagogy by focusing on a much needed area of work within teacher education: addressing the influence of media discourses on Islam in teacher education. Amina Shareef and Adrien Chauvet discuss how since 9/11, dominant media streams propagate an essentialized image of Islam that conjures associations of violence, fanaticism, and barbarity. They argue that the implications of these media discourses penetrate the public, legal, and private spheres and attempt to explicate the consequences of this penetration. They posit that the perpetuation of such discourses erodes the possibility for democratic engagement and subsequently propose possible interventions such as teacher education programs that schools can deploy in providing counterdiscourses to Mass Media Islam—the media's version of Islam. The authors conclude by marking the urgency of scholastic intervention for creating mutual respect and reciprocity among followers of different faiths and spiritualities in an increasingly religiously diverse society.

In Chapter 6, "Identity and Social Justice Development of Preservice Teachers," Maricela Alvarado and Amy Carey explore a social justice identity development theory intended to enhance preservice curricula and challenge preservice educators to raise self-awareness of their racial biases, personal histories, privileges, and identities by examining themselves personally. They argue that self-reflection, awareness of their privilege, and confidence in preservice teachers' own social justice identity development seems to be the foundation of what could possibly address the other situational factors. They discuss a preservice development theory based on culturally relevant pedagogy, student leadership development, and White and ethnic identity development theories. They use processes of self-awareness/privilege, reflection/inquiry, action, and continual inquiry as the developmental tools of this theory. They suggest, and further outline, the following stages for preservice development: (a) internal place or level of awareness, (b) external (structural) awareness, and (c) reflection for continual inquiry and action. They conclude with a theory of social justice identity development for preservice teachers that provides a conceptual base for preservice educators on how to teach for social justice while supporting their students' development and growth.

Chapter 7, "A Social Justice Curriculum for Appalachia," develops a dimension of curriculum and pedagogy specific to teacher preparation in Appalachia. Ryan Angus and Joshus Iddings examine various discourses about education in the central Appalachian region. They present the largely negative historical representations of education in Appalachia—both the educational system and its students. Because many of these negative representations and stereotypes persist in Appalachia today, they look at the transformative role that teacher educators and teachers can play in the region. In order to bring about this transformation, they propose a curriculum for Appalachia that incorporates historical texts, literature, student writing, and service learning. This critical focus on literature, writing, and service would teach preservice teachers, teachers, and students to be more critical citizens who seek out solutions to problems in their local contexts.

Contexts, Structures, and Collaborators

This dimension highlights candidates' learning with more experienced mentors engaged in university-school partnerships who are themselves working with others in inquiry communities that foster equity and access. It further emphasizes the roles of parents, families, and community groups, especially those from historically marginalized groups, as collaborators in teacher preparation (Cochran-Smith, 2010). The chapter that addresses this dimension describes a university-community partnership focused on preparing prospective teachers to serve as agents in Latino/a children's literacy development.

Chapter 8, "*Al Otro Lado del Puente:* Fostering Partnerships Literacy Between Academia and the Latino/a Community," emphasizes that teacher preparation includes working within communities as collaborators. Zaira R. Arvelo Alicea and Ileana Cortés Santiago describe their experiences working with Latino/a families and prospective teachers in the development and implementation of a small-scale community engagement project sponsored by a university-based grant. The main goal of this project was to highlight the importance of preparing prospective teachers to serve as agents in Latino/a children's literacy development. First, they discuss their involvement in this project as foregrounded by their experiences growing up in a Latino/a community in the Caribbean and their current research foci as doctoral students. Second, they present a model for promoting literacy development based on the remarkable work carried out by a Puerto Rican social agent. Then, they explain the conception of social justice that undergirds this project, which focuses on two tenets: family involvement and culturally sensitive curricula. They conclude by offering brief accounts of the events carried out in two venues to elucidate the implementation of their proposed literacy development model and their conception of social justice.

Outcomes

This dimension addresses teacher preparation for justice that promotes student learning and is responsible for both teacher and student learning. It highlights the need to guarantee that all students have rich opportunities to learn, giving consideration to the current state of accountability systems and working toward challenging test and curriculum content (Cochran-Smith, 2010). The chapters in this section address this dimension by focusing on challenging inequities to ensure that all students have rich opportunities to learn and reject the notion that scores on standardized tests are the sole measure of students' academic success.

In Chapter 9, "Preparing Mathematics Teachers for Culturally and Linguistically Diverse Students: What's Language Got to Do With Social Justice?," David Norris and Luciana C. de Oliveira explore the preparation of mathematics teachers to work with culturally and linguistically diverse students. They address the relationship between language and mathematics and add to current understandings of the role of language in mathematics to focus specifically on preparing mathematics teachers for social justice work through a focus on developing their understanding of language in mathematics learning. The goal of their work is to challenge inequities by ensuring that all students have rich opportunities to learn mathematics, not just opportunities to be held accountable to the same high stakes, and show that language can be a key gatekeeper in mathematics learning.

Also focused on mathematics, Chapter 10, "Mathematics + Social Justice = A New Take on Mathematics Teacher Preparation," addresses an application of theories of social justice in mathematics. Caitlyn Holleran and Kadriye El-Atwani outline a hypothetical course for preservice mathematics teachers that any mathematics teacher education program could implement. The main goal of the course is to connect social justice theory to practice in the mathematics classroom. In conjunction with a mathematics classroom field experience, this course will have students study the theories that undergird social justice and complete assignments and activities for their field experience classroom that are rooted in social justice principles. A course like the one they describe here will give beginning mathematics teachers the tools to effectively integrate social justice into their own teaching, with a result of enhanced learning among *all* students. The proposed course includes a wide range of academic, social, emotional, civic, and life skills and rejects the notion that scores on standardized tests are the only measure of students' success in mathematics.

In Chapter 11, "The Unintended Consequences of No Child Left Behind on an Indiana School Corporation: Implications for English Language Learners' Advocates," April M. Burke reports on a study that investigated the impact of No Child Left Behind (NCLB) on a rural Indiana school corporation in which English language learners make up over 26% of the student population. Through interviews with three administrators and an analysis of student test performance, the study highlights a number of issues that must be addressed if the stated goal of NCLB's Title I to close existing achievement gaps is to be met. The chapter includes implications for teachers, administrators, and other advocates who seek to address the unintended consequences of NCLB for schools with diverse populations.

TEACHER EDUCATION FOR SOCIAL JUSTICE:
PERSPECTIVES AND LESSONS LEARNED

As can be grasped from the above chapters' descriptions, this book addresses different perspectives about the preparation of teachers for social justice work. The preparation of teachers with the knowledge, dispositions, and practices to work with culturally and linguistically diverse students is a key responsibility of teacher education (Cochran-Smith, 2004; McDonald & Zeichner, 2009). The title of this book, *Teacher Education for Social Justice: Perspectives and Lessons Learned*, highlights some important aspects of the work presented here. The book focuses on *teacher education for social justice* and offers multiple *perspectives* on several key areas that can be addressed in teacher education programs. The phrase *lessons learned* is used because the volume grew out of a course focused on the topics discussed in each one of the chapters. After carefully examining current and relevant developments in social justice teacher education, the authors offer suggestions for teacher education programs that aim to incorporate a social justice focus.

REFERENCES

Agarwal, R., Epstein, S., Oppenheim, R., Oyler, C., & Sonu, D. (2010). From ideal to practice and back again: Beginning teachers teaching for social justice. *Journal of Teacher Education, 61*(3), 237–247.

Athanases, S. Z., & de Oliveira, L. C. (2008). Advocacy for equity in classrooms and beyond: New teachers' challenges and responses. *Teachers College Record, 110*(1), 64–104.

Athanases, S. Z., & de Oliveira, L. C. (2010). Toward program-wide coherence in preparing teachers to teach and advocate for English language learners. In T. Lucas (Ed.), *Teacher preparation for linguistically diverse classrooms: A resource for teacher educators* (pp. 195–215). New York, NY: Routledge.

Banks, J. (2002). Race, knowledge construction, and education in the USA: Lessons from history. *Race, Ethnicity and Education, 5*(1), 7–27.

Chubbuck, S. M. (2010). Individual and structural orientations in socially just teaching: Conceptualization, implementation, and collaborative work. *Journal of Teacher Education, 61*(3), 197–210.

Cochran-Smith, M. (2004). *Walking the road: Race, diversity, and social justice in teacher education.* New York, NY: Teachers College Press.

Cochran-Smith, M. (2010). Toward a theory of teacher education for social justice. In A. Hargreaves et al. (Eds.), *Second international handbook of educational change* (pp. 445–467). New York, NY: Springer.

Cochran-Smith, M., Barnatt, J., Lahann, R., Shakman, K., & Terrell, D. (2009). Teacher education for social justice: Critiquing the critiques. In W. Ayers, T. Quinn, & D. Stovall (Eds.), *Handbook of social justice in education* (pp. 625–639). New York, NY: Routledge.

Darling-Hammond, L. (2010). Teacher education and the American future. *Journal of Teacher Education, 6*(1/2), 35–47.

de Oliveira, L. C., & Athanases, S. Z. (2007). Graduates' reports of advocating for English language learners. *Journal of Teacher Education, 58*(3), 202–215.

Freire, P. (2000). *Pedagogy of the oppressed.* New York, NY: Continuum.

McDonald, M. (2005). The integration of social justice in teacher education: Dimensions of prospective teachers' opportunities to learn. *Journal of Teacher Education, 56*(5), 418–435.

McDonald, M. (2007). The joint enterprise of social justice teacher education. *Teachers College Record, 109*(8), 2047–2081.

McDonald, M., & Zeichner, K. (2009). Social justice teacher education. In W. Ayers, T. Quinn, & D. Stovall (Eds.), *Handbook of social justice in education* (pp. 595–610). New York, NY: Routledge.

Zeichner, Z. (2009). *Teacher education and the struggle for social justice.* New York, NY: Routledge.

CHAPTER 2

SOCIALLY JUST TEACHING THROUGH THE EYES OF RUSSIAN IMMIGRANTS

Galina Miller and Lyubov Sylayeva

The concept of social justice has challenged theorists for decades, generating numerous definitions and arguments. Indeed, what is social justice? What does this concept mean in regard to teaching and teacher education?

Generally, social justice refers to the fairness of a society in its divisions and distributions of rewards or opportunities, in spite of identifying characteristics such as race, class, gender, ability, or language (Chubbuck, 2010). One of the social justice constructs originates from the liberal democratic theory, a distributive paradigm that has guided theories of justice for half of the last century. It focuses on the equal opportunities of individuals, civic involvement, and a common political dedication to the autonomy of all citizens to accomplish their own version of a fulfilling life (Cochran-Smith, 2010). From this standpoint, social justice is achieved through the "redistribution of material and other goods, power, and access with the goal of establishing society based on fairness and equality" (Cochran-Smith, 2010, p. 450). An alternative view of social justice focuses on the politics of identity and individual differences and was formed by the contemporary political

Teacher Education for Social Justice: Perspectives and Lessons Learned, pages 11–22.
Copyright © 2013 by Information Age Publishing

11

philosophy. It states that in today's diverse society, it is essential to respect and recognize all social groups constructed on culture, race, gender, religious beliefs, language, ability/disability, and sexual orientation.

It is important to note that social justice is interwoven with multicultural education. According to McDonald and Zeichner (2009), social justice developed out of "almost 30 years of effort within teacher education to include multicultural education" (p. 596). The main purpose of multicultural education is to enhance the educational opportunities and knowledge of English language learners, students of color, special needs, low-income, and students deemed "at risk." Furthermore, McDonald and Zeichner emphasize that social justice in teacher education concentrates more on issues of social justice, while multicultural education gives much attention to the issues of cultural diversity. Thus, there is a strong connection between social justice and multicultural education.

SOCIAL JUSTICE IN THE CLASSROOM: TEACHING AND LEARNING

The meaning of social justice is individualistic and is strongly linked to national and cultural heritage. Rubin (2010) asserts that there is an enormous gap in the implementation of social justice principles into teacher education programs between developing nations and developed countries. This is primarily due to the fact that social and political systems in which teachers live, study, and work shape their views. Thus, the issues of social justice in Afghanistan are different from those of the United States. Afghan students, especially girls who lived under the Taliban regime, did not have the opportunity to attend schools. In fact, many women were not only severely limited in their rights, but frequently suffered from physical and mental abuse. Therefore, teacher education under the Taliban regime could not provide even elementary civil rights to all Afghan people.

In many places, teaching social justice has to be a strictly personal decision that requires strong dedication on the part of the educator. This is especially true when a teacher risks constant prosecution and the possibility of being criminally punished for teaching and practicing social justice in the classroom. Under these circumstances, teachers must have an extreme amount of courage to discuss the highly controversial issues of oppression and social, racial, cultural, and economic justice with students. However, strong dedication is not enough; teachers must also possess the knowledge of social justice principles, which they may have never experienced themselves. Thus, it is crucial to find ways of effectively sharing social justice norms with teachers worldwide. Multicultural communication has the potential to greatly influence our ability to embrace social justice in our academic systems. According to Cochran-Smith (2004), the "goal of teacher education is to make it normative rather than exceptional for teachers and teacher educators to work as advocates for social justice" (p. 23). When social justice theory becomes normative in education, its constructs can expand beyond the classroom, eventually creating a more just global society.

As educators, we are able to bring change to the existing "norms." This idea is supported by Kumashiro's (2002) philosophy, which states that educators must be responsible and committed to the process of learning and teaching, as well as engaged in anti-oppressive education. Through practicing this philosophy, we "participate in the ongoing, never-completed construction of knowledge" (p. 44) and help our children learn the fundamentals of social justice through observation. As Galina reflects on her teaching experience in Russia, she states,

> When I think back about the behavior of my students, I can equate them to sponges, who absorb and perceive the teacher's attitudes and subliminal messages, many of which may be sent unintentionally. Thus, to make schooling more effective, educators should have to create and follow an oath, such as the Oath of Hypocrites, with the basic principle to avoid harming others. As educators, we must respect our students' cultural capital and understand the theory of personal identity, in order to protect the student's sense of self and to form a diverse and empowering learning environment.

The key tenant of social justice in education is to promote equal opportunities to all students in receiving a quality education while respecting the civil rights and cultural diversity of each individual. However, in order to effectively promote equality in the classroom, one must first become familiar with the extant social injustice issues. Although political and social issues can have a profound influence on a teacher's perception of social justice, personal experiences can play an equally important role. Teachers who come from diverse communities or a lower socioeconomic status may have experienced inequities and struggles throughout their lives. However, these experiences may ultimately increase their awareness and understanding of social justice issues, making these teachers better adapted to encourage equality in their own classroom.

The principles gained from experience are difficult to teach in the classroom. One of the most pressing questions in today's teacher education is, How can the principles and experiences of social justice be instilled in preservice teachers who grew up in a homogenous society, with limited experiences with inequities, racial diversity, and multicultural exposure? Chubbuck (2010) promotes the idea of acquiring the necessary skills and knowledge through individual self-reflection on issues of injustice. She indicates that teachers should "learn to see outside of blinders of their personal racial, cultural, or socioeconomic experience to identify how structurally imposed privilege and discrimination have affected both them and their students' lives" (p. 204).

Reflecting on her educational experience, Lyubov pointed out,

During my primary education, in the U.S.S.R., I experienced little diversity, with classes consisting of strictly Russian students. Despite the fact that the Soviet Union consisted of fifteen republics, it was difficult and costly to travel throughout the nation, with only a small segment of the population being able to afford it. As a result, our teachers lacked the experience of working with a diverse population. However, each year the entire school organized a festival to celebrate the cultures of all fifteen republics. It was through these festivals, particularly when I was given an assignment to make a traditional dress worn by women in the former Tajik Soviet Republic, which I became aware of and interested in learning more about other cultures and their traditions. Now the nation of Tajikistan, it is a mountainous and distant country in Central Asia, with the majority of the population belonging to the Persian-speaking ethnic group, similar to Iran and Afghanistan in language and culture. As I began learning about the Tajik culture, I was surprised by the diversity and uniqueness of the traditional attire; for instance, Tajik girls not only had remarkable clothes but also an extraordinary culture that appeared strict, mysterious and at the same time fascinating. As I learned more about this region, I became aware of the stern norms and the discrimination against women. These findings caused me to reflect on my own place in the world and to compare the social and political issues that existed world-wide.

This example illustrates that the need to increase teacher awareness and exposure to cultural, racial, and social diversity is not unique to the United States alone. One method that could help facilitate preservice teacher comprehension concerning issues of diversity in education is through immersion in different cultural and language environments by participation in study-abroad programs. At the present time, many teacher education programs have begun to value the importance of such experiences. Study-abroad programs can also be specifically tailored to expose prospective teachers to racial or socioeconomic diversity. According to Phillion et al. (2008) the goal of such programs is to "develop the ability to work with diverse students and to recognize the implications of social justice issues for teaching" (p. 367). For example, during such a program in Honduras, teachers were strongly encouraged to immerse themselves in the local culture and the lives of their students and asked students to work together with parents and the community. Participating preservice teachers experienced "hands-on" task learning, working in the local school, reading and discussing topics related to multicultural issues, and contributing to the daily life of the community.

Similarly, in order to enhance teaching methods and pedagogy, Chubbuck (2010) suggests assigning "pre-service teachers in racially, culturally, and socioeconomically diverse field placement, where their theoretical knowledge and structural orientation in their professional reflection can be put into practice" (p. 205). Furthermore, Chubbuck emphasizes the importance of university supervisor support to preservice teachers. In addition to personal experiences and the support of supervisors, a meaningful and structured curriculum that "includes controversial topics and possible student responses on a role-play of various stakeholders each with different position" (p. 206) can increase exposure and therefore raise awareness of various social justice issues.

Multicultural and social justice courses should also be incorporated into teacher education programs in order to allow future teachers to explore the issues of equality in the classroom even further. McDonald and Zeichner (2009) propose a goal of using "various instructional strategies in teacher education courses to expand the sociocultural consciousness of prospective teachers" (p. 604). Incorporating field experiences into teacher education can help preservice teachers understand and familiarize themselves with "the structures and social networks that exist in the communities where their pupils live" (p. 604). Teaching in urban public schools is a great opportunity to improve urban education and to make a difference in the lives of many students. In addition, it can help preservice teachers gain valuable experience while working under a novel set of conditions. For instance, the majority of prospective teachers have no personal experience dealing with problems that many students from low-income backgrounds experience daily. Thus, working in low-income schools allows teachers to prepare to resolve multiple racial, gender, sexual, diversity, and religious issues. According to Lee, Eckrich, Lackey, & Showalter (2010), "hands-on community-based, immersive activities, combined with structured opportunities for critical reflection, provide students with powerful tools for examining and possibly rethinking of redrawing their cultural maps regarding teaching underserved urban areas and in variously diverse classrooms" (p. 117). The goal of social justice in education is to provide students with an equal opportunity to receive a quality education, regardless of the income, race, or gender.

Another way to create positive change in teacher education programs is through bringing change to the "demographic imperative" through hiring faculty and students of color of varied socioeconomic backgrounds and international origin, as it is essential to alter the disproportions in the educational system. Zeichner (2009) emphasizes that "a diverse learning community in teacher education programs is critical to our ability to prepare teachers for diverse schools" (p. 19). He claims that we need to prepare teachers for culturally diverse and high-poverty schools. Many universities in the United States are changing admission requirements from those that were primarily centered on academic achievements to criteria that are more focused on personal experiences and racial diversity.

It must be pointed out that many social and economic limitations exist that prevent these groups from entering the education profession. The educational system in the United States attempts to provide equal educational opportunities to all children; however, these attempts often fail, thus reinforcing and replicating injustice (Apple, 2006).

Currently, many public urban schools in the United States are experiencing severe difficulties due to limited government support. As a result, minority and low-income students struggle to acquire a basic quality education and suffer from cyclical low achievement in major content areas of education. The inability to meet standard education requirements restricts many of these students from pursing a university education and consequently improving their lives and their family's socioeconomic status. In order to encourage students of color or low income to pursue the teaching profession, government and federal financial aid, and college and university funds should be available for such students, and their education tuition costs should remain low.

Society and schools have to make a concerted effort to reference the pattern of academic failure, in which educators and students must confront historical models of disempowerment. These patterns are characterized by the idea that those who have political power and control over society use the educational institutions to implement the ideologies, aligned with their own beliefs (e.g., Apple, 2006; Ayers, 2001; Counts, 2009; Green 2009; Noddings, 2009). Thus, the political, ideological, economic, and social issues are interwoven throughout the history of teacher education in a pattern that preserves the status quo (Cummins, 1996).

THE NEED FOR A MULTICULTURAL APPROACH

According to Nieto (2002), during the last two decades, there has been a colossal boost in the number of immigrants entering the United States. This abrupt influx has left many educators struggling to assist students in U.S. schools, as they "increasingly come from a variety of economic, linguistic, cultural and ethnic backgrounds" (de Oliveira & Athanases, 2007, p. 202). These children bring diverse experiences and potentials. Valdes (1998) notes that in the process of moving to the United States, immigrant children and their families have to "travel long distances," which has a "physical, emotional, and psychological" impact (p. 174). According to the National Center of Educational Statistics (2002), with rapid changes in student demographics, the majority of teachers and future educators feel unprepared for teaching English language learners (ELLs). The lack of experience in teaching under diverse circumstances can lead immigrant and minority children to experience culturally based conflicts, identity negotiation, prejudice, and discrimination. As a result, ELL students chronically fall behind their native English speakers and experience higher dropout rates. Thus, as educators, we must improve our capacity to better assist immigrants and minority students with acquiring a second language and adapting to the mainstream culture without losing their own identities.

A body of literature that deals with the facilitation of second language acquisition suggests that psychological emotions (i.e., anxiety, motivation, and self-confidence) play a major role in learning a second language. Krashen (1982) states that these variables may strongly increase or restrain second language acquisition. Lucas, Villegas, & Freedson-Gonzalez (2008) advocate that "a safe, welcoming environment with minimum anxiety about performing in a second language is essential for ELLs to learn" (p. 364). However, educational institutions can often cause ELLs and minority students to experience anxiety, discouragement, and humiliation (Lucas et al., 2008). This is particularly important because acquiring a second language requires individual to obtain another identity (Krashen, 1982). One's identity is cultivated through interaction, and language is a significant medium in personal relations, becoming pivotal to the perception of self. Replacing an individual's sense of self is psychologically challenging, particularly when it is challenged in the academic environment.

In Galina's reflection on her personal experience, she comments,

> Ironically, the value and realization of my own identity occurred in the process of straying away from my native language and culture. I was born and raised in the former U.S.S.R., a heterogeneous nation, comprised of 165 different nationalities and fifteen autonomous republics, each with their unique languages, religious beliefs, customs, and traditions. My ancestors were Mari by nationality and belonged to the Fino-Ugric tribes that formed the Mari El republic. The official languages in the region are Russian and Mari, however, the only language taught in the urban areas was Russian, with both languages taught only in the rural areas. However, growing up a Mari-Russian brought complications to my life. Throughout my elementary education, my Mari culture was never explored or discussed in the classroom. Furthermore, the context the Russian language was promoted while the Mari language was discouraged and mocked, especially among children. I became ashamed of my identity, as children used to tease and call me names. I felt like an outsider to the both cultures and experienced inner conflict. As a result of juggling my identities, I became shy and tried not to attract attention to myself, to avoid ridicule. I think my experiences as a culturally diverse student were not discrete from other Mari students.

One's own understanding of personal identity is the combination of unique features an individual possesses, interwoven with race, class, gender, religion, custom, tradition, ability, and language. The core of self-esteem is in one's interpersonal competence in communication. According to Schumann (1986), stated second language learners go through "language shock," a phobia of being mocked when trying to interact in a second language (p. 382). The learner's feelings to elude extra attention, in combination with embarrassment and criticism anxiety, may serve to decline their English language acquisition and to master course contents. The fear and confusion that ELLs face in inflowing another culture, which is known as "cultural shock," can increase complications in the process of education for such students. ELLs require assistance in becoming full participants of the education process rather than passive audience members. Support and respect can effectively help students to cultivate better interactive abilities in English, thus increasing their enthusiasm and academic accomplishments. Thus, the role of the teacher is extremely important in ensuring that students can reach their full potential without losing their sense of identity and self in the process.

THE ROLE OF THE TEACHER

Recent research on student achievement validates that educators have a direct impact on the quality of education and student scholastic achievements (Ayers, 2001; Valdes, 1998; Valenzuela, 1999). Evidence in the literature suggests that a student whose culture is respected and voiced in the classroom will have positive self-esteem and motivation for success, thus education becomes meaningful to him/her. Teachers are at the center of this transformation. Cummins (1996) asserts that students and teachers need to establish trust and respect in order for learning to take place. Schooling is deeply rooted in human relationships because students formulate, broaden, and confirm their sense of self through peer and teacher-student interactions. Teaching is an ongoing, two-way process in which they educate and are educated by the students. It is a process that keeps teachers "alive"—intellectually engaged, involved, curious, and continuously learning. Nothing is static in the classroom, and the everyday environment is a living element. Often, success in teaching depends on the educator's attitude toward her/ himself, and his/her inherent feelings toward the students, regardless of the student's social, cultural, or racial distinctions.

Culturally relevant pedagogies must be able to create suitable conditions for students to form a negotiated identity, an identity that overlaps both with the culture of origin and the school culture. This must be done in a way that does not require the loss of one's uniqueness for academic achievement, because identities are unstable and are not inherent, but fluid and adaptive (Moje & Luke, 2009). Students' identities are produced and reproduced through social interactions, thus it is the educators' task to realize that their engagement in authentic relationships with students is critical to shaping the students' identities and emphasizing academic self-confidence. This is particularly salient for ELLs, because students with identities positioned in a minority culture must see reflections of themselves in the learning process in order to realize a negotiated identity that allows them to excel in school while maintaining their cultural individuality.

Our task as educators is to determine ways of create an appealing educational atmosphere and encouraging students' active involvement within the academic setting so that language learners and mainstream students attain the complete and meaningful communication and benefits in cooperation. A variety of tools and strategies can be used for this purpose. Lucas et al. (2008) asserts that using extralinguistic supports, such as visual tools (i.e., pictures, illustration, maps, videos, graphs, timelines, Venn diagrams) can be helpful in increasing comprehension and fostering participation in students with limited language skills. Other strategies, such as supplementing and modifying oral language, engaging students in peer interactions, facilitating and encouraging the use of students' mother tongue, can be effective in improving communication in a diverse classroom.

Conflicts of association with the English language and mainstream culture, often experienced by immigrants, play a significant role in the educational process and can be addressed by integrating them into the academic curriculum. This can be done through designing classroom activities (student's projects and culture circles) that focus on topics of adaptation and welcome students to share and value their own individual experience, use of native language, especially in course subjects such as behavioral and social science, literature, and English as a second language.

A give-and-take communication paradigm promotes a system of significant verbal and written interactions among educators and students as the positive academic environment. Students' presentations, projects, and classroom debates add to the traditional teacher's lecture format. Lucas et al. (2008) stressed that "linguistic and academic skills that are developed in one's native language can transfer to a second language and thus serve as rich resources for learning in that language" (p. 366). According to Cummins (2000), a "transmission" pedagogy model eliminates and restrains the students' personal experience from the academic setting in order to make a one-way "pipeline" of knowledge from the educator to the students. In this method, the instructor submissively transfers, the students obediently receive, and the school authorities manipulate the learning process by reducing students' participation and involvement, thus the communication principle of the language gets lost. On the other hand, experimental pedagogy seeks to integrate the students' cultural and language backgrounds into the academic setting to recognize students' linguistic and cultural experiences and to invigorate their active involvement in the classroom. Therefore, recognition of diverse students' cultural capital becomes a potent device for actively engaging English language learners in a meaningful process of education.

CONCLUSION

The definition of social justice in education strives to provide equal opportunities to all students, in spite of race, class, gender, ability, or language. Practicing social justice requires the knowledge of cultural and racial inequalities that exist today. This is often difficult for teachers who have limited experience working with diverse groups of students; however the need for experienced teachers is growing as classroom diversity increases. Thus, various immersion and study-abroad programs can help better prepare teachers to assist minority students in reaching their maximum potential and become active members of society.

Educators play a direct role in the quality of education and student academic achievement. ELL's language and culture shock often prevent them from actively engaging in the education process. Teachers have to find ways of promoting active student participation so that both second language learners and native speakers can form an effective learning environment. Therefore, it is critical to empower the minority and immigrant students through (a) incorporation of the student culture into the classroom setting, (b) collaboration with parents, and (c) encouragement of the use of both native and second languages. Educators should work to prevent academic and cultural losses among students from minority groups through empowerment and the exploration of cultural diversity. As educators, we have the unique opportunity to enact social justice, a demanding and powerful role, which comes with the constant obligation to be advocates of our students and to treat them fairly and equitably regardless of background or privilege.

REFERENCES

Apple, M. (2006). Interrupting the right: On doing critical educational work in conservative times. In G. Ladson-Billings & W. Tate (Eds.), *Educational research in the public interest: Social justice, action, and policy* (pp. 27–45). New York, NY: Teachers College Press.

Ayers, W. (2001). *To teach: The journey of a teacher.* New York, NY and London, UK: Teachers College Press.

Chubbuck, S. M. (2010). Individual and structural orientations in socially just teaching: Conceptualization, implementation, collaborative effort. *Journal of Teacher Education, 61*(3), 197–210.

Cochran-Smith, M. (2004). *Walking the road: Race, diversity, and social justice in teacher education.* New York, NY: Teachers College Press.

Cochran-Smith, M. (2010). Toward a theory of teacher education for social justice. In A. Hargreaves et al. (Eds), *Second international handbook of educational change* (pp. 445–464). Springer Science+Business Media B.V.2010.

Counts, G. (2009). Dare the schools build a new social order? In D. J. Flinders & S. J. Thornton (Eds.), *The curriculum studies reader* (pp. 45–51). New York: Routledge.

Cummins, J. (1996). *Negotiating identities: Education for empowerment in a diverse society.* Ontario, CA: CABE.

Cummins, J. (2000). *Language, power, and pedagogy: Bilingual children at the crossfire.* Clevedon, UK: Multilingual Matters.

de Oliveira, L. C., & Athanases, S. Z. (2007). Graduates' reports of advocating for English language learners. *Journal of Teacher Education,58,* 202–215

Freire, P. (2009). Pedagogy of the oppressed. In D. J. Flinders & S. J. Thornton (Eds.), *The curriculum studies reader* (3rd ed., pp. 147–154). New York, NY: Routledge.

Green, M. (2009). Curriculum and consciousness. In D. J. Flinders & S. J. Thornton (Eds.), *The curriculum studies reader* (pp. 55–167). New York: Routledge.

Kumashiro, K. K. (2002) Toward a theory of anti-oppressive education. *Review of Educational Research,* Spring 2000, (701), 25–53.

Lee, R. E., Eckrich, L. L., Lackey, C., & Showalter, B. D. (2010). Pre-service teacher pathways to urban teaching: A partnership model nurturing community-based urban teacher preparation. *Teacher Education Quarterly, 37*(3), 101–122.

Lucas, T., Villegas, A. M., & Freedson-Gonzalez, M. (2008). Linguistically responsive teacher education. *Journal of Teacher Education, 59*(4), 361–373

McDonald, M., & Zeichner, K. M. (2009). Social justice teacher education. In W. Ayers, T. Quinn, & D. Stovall (Eds.), *Handbook of social justice in education* (pp. 595–610). New York, NY: Routledge.

Moje, E. B., & Luke, A. (2009). Literacy and identity: Examining the metaphors in history and contemporary research. *Reading Research Quarterly, 44,* 415–437.

National Center for Educational Statistics. (2002). *1999–2000 schools and staffing survey, Overview of the data for public, private, public charter and bureau of Indian affairs elementary and secondary schools.* Washington, DC: U.S. Department of Education, Office of Educational Research and Improvement.

Nieto, S. (2002). *Language, culture, teaching: Critical perspectives for a new century.* Mahwah: NJ: Lawrence Erlbaum.

Noddings, N. (2009). The false promise of the Paideia: A critical review of The Paideia Proposal. In D. J. Flinders & S. J. Thornton (Eds.), *The curriculum studies reader* (pp. 180–187). New York: Routledge.

Phillion, J., Malewski, E., Rodriguez, E., Shirley, V., Kulago, H., & Bulington, J. (2008). Promise and perils of study abroad. White privilege revival. In T. Huber–Warring (Ed.), *Growing a soul for social change: Building the knowledge base for social justice* (pp. 365–382). Charlotte, NC: Information Age Publishing.

Rubin, E. (2010). Veiled rebellion. *National Geographic, 218,* 28–53.

Schumann, J. (1986). Research on the acculturation model for second language acquisition. *Journal of Multilingual and Multicultural Development, 7,* 379–392.

Valenzuela, A. (1999). Subtractive schooling U.S.—Mexican youth and the politics of caring. New York: State University of New York Press.

Valdés, G (1998). The world outside and inside schools: Language and immigrant children. *Educational Researcher, 27*(6), 4–18.

Valdés, G. (2001). *Learning and not learning English: Latino students in American schools.* New York: Teachers College Press.

Zeichner, K. M. (2009). *Teacher education and the struggle for social justice.* New York, NY: Routledge.

CHAPTER 3

TEACHER EDUCATION FOR IMMIGRANT STUDENTS:

The Educational Issues of Immigrant Students in the United States and Japan

Thu Ya Aung, Shaivi Divatia, and Reiko Akiyama

The United States continues to attract immigrants from various countries, each with their own racial, cultural, and linguistic diversities. Consequently, immigrant children with diverse languages, cultures, and races often face inequalities in the classroom, which is a problem for both educators and immigrant children. Teachers may not always be aware of the immigrant childrens' cultures and identities and may not be prepared to teach immigrant students. Southern states in particular are facing a shortage of teachers who can teach immigrant English language learners, and teacher education programs generally fail to adequately deal with designing curricula for addressing this group of students. The assimilation process for the children of immigrants poses several educational challenges not only for the immigrants but also for the educational establishment.

Immigrant children commonly face issues such as educational inequity, language barriers, and resistance to being accepted by the existing popula-

Teacher Education for Social Justice: Perspectives and Lessons Learned, pages 23–34.
Copyright © 2013 by Information Age Publishing
23

tion. These issues are not only seen in the United States but are also rising rapidly internationally, including the racially homogeneous country of Japan. Recently, more people have been immigrating to Japan. The Japanese education system has several issues, such as the issue of teacher education for immigrant students, language barrier issues, an achievement gap, and reduced involvement from parents of immigrant children.

In this chapter, we will discuss the elements that are needed in teacher education programs to help better serve immigrant children by discussing prominent issues in both the United States and Japan. We include suggestions to address ongoing issues in both countries.

Social justice in teacher education refers to promoting equality in the education system by eliminating racial, class, language, and gender discrimination (Cochran-Smith, 2003, 2004; McDonald & Zeichner, 2009; Zeichner, 2009). Teaching is one of the noblest professions, and teachers are potentially in a position to literally change the world (Vadivelu, 2007). Education is a right for all children irrespective of differences in gender, class, socioeconomic status, or race. In the United States, the No Child Left Behind Act, passed in 2001, has led teachers to focus more on standardized tests. Likewise, the current Japanese educational system strongly regards test scores as important; this emphasis marginalizes many immigrant students because of their lower achievements (Nakada & Muramatsu, 2006; Tamaki, Harada, & Wakabayashi, 2009). In this chapter, we discuss several issues related to social justice in teacher education, especially focusing on the issues related to immigrant students in the United States and Japan.

ISSUES OF IMMIGRANT EDUCATION IN THE UNITED STATES

There has been a sharp increase in immigration to the United States since 2000 (Garcia, 2005). The foreign-born population was 12.5% of the total population in 2008 (U.S. Census Bureau, 2011). In the years 1999–2000, seven states experienced over a 100% increase in the children of immigrants attending pre-K through fifth grade (Garcia, Arias, Harris Murri, & Serna, 2010). In 2008, approximately 5.1 % of students enrolled in elementary and high schools were foreign-born, and 17.1% were native citizens with at least one foreign-born parent (U.S. Census Bureau, 2011). With an increase in the number of immigrant students, certain issues have become prevalent in public education in the United States.

Teachers' Lack of Preparation for Immigrant Education

Most public school teachers are predominantly White and learned English as their first language (Howard, 2007). In 2007–2008, there were 2,829,000 White teachers in the United States while their Black and Hispanic counterparts numbered 239,000 and 240,000, respectively (U.S. Census

Bureau, 2011). White teachers have often had very little opportunity to experience a culture different from their own (Davis, Ramahlo, Beyerbach, & London, 2008) and are often unaware of the needs of immigrant children, who are predominantly English language learners (ELLs) in the process of learning English (Valdes, 1998).

Most of the immigrant students may still need to learn English; therefore, another crucial aspect of immigrant education is teaching ELLs. In 2008, approximately 20.5 % of all 5–17-year-old children in the United States were users of another language at home (U.S. Census Bureau, 2011). In addition, English language learners often struggle with high-stakes testing (Solorzano, 2008). To succeed in schools in the United States, immigrant students need to understand and read their texts and understand their peers and teachers completely "in English." Southern states are facing a shortage of teachers who can teach ELLs, but many teacher education programs throughout the country do not offer bilingual education preparation or address only minimally the challenge of teaching ELLs (Sox, 2009; Wainer, 2004). According to Sox (2009), teacher education programs fail to adequately deal with key content for English as a second language (ESL) and bilingual content such as linguistics, sociolinguistics and second language acquisition, culturally and linguistically relevant pedagogies, and choosing appropriate materials and assessments. In a study about immigrant education, Wainer (2004) found that "respondents inside and outside the school system agree that the lack of ESL and bilingual trained teachers is a major barrier to immigrant educational success" (p. 26). The shortage of ESL and bilingual teachers becomes a major hurdle for the education of immigrants and one that needs serious consideration.

Teacher Preparation for Immigrant Students in the United States

Preservice teachers must be prepared to welcome immigrant students in the classroom and make the environment inviting for all students (Lucas, Villegas, & Freedson-Gonzalez, 2008). One way to achieve this goal is to allow children to speak more than one language. Studies have shown that immigrant children who speak more than one language in school in the United States perform better in school (Levels, Dronkers, & Kraaykamp, 2008). Adequately trained, licensed, and qualified teachers are necessary for immigrant children to have equal opportunities in school (Chu, 2009).

Teacher preparation must reflect the current situation in the United States. It becomes important for preservice teachers to take advantage of "opportunities to explore and comprehend their own cultural and personal values, their identities, and their social belief" to understand the word "diversity" (Garcia et al., 2010, p. 136). One of the major necessities is to hire multicultural teachers to help the immigrant children settle into their new environment and acquire a sense of belonging to the community.

Also, preservice teacher diversity programs need to offer more components such as finding ways to increase accessibility for minority students and immigrants, involving communication with parents and upgrading the curriculum so that the teaching can be made culturally responsive to students (Cruickshank, 2004). One important way to implement culturally responsive teaching is to involve families in school programs and in classroom activities in order for the teachers to better understand the student's cultural background (Grant & Gillette, 2006). Given the ever-diversifying dynamic of U.S. public schools, the paradigm of culturally responsive teaching is necessary to the success of all schools.

Oikonomidoy (2011) discussed implications specifically for teacher education while advocating immigrant-responsive multicultural education. In addition to training in bilingual education, teachers should be prepared to understand migration from multidisciplinary points of view through "specific courses on immigration and education." Moreover, teacher education should expand multicultural education courses to encompass global issues that could focus on "intercultural exchanges and experiences." Consequently, teachers will develop intercultural awareness and "immigrant-responsive(ness)" (p. 28).

It is also important for preservice teachers to be actively involved in the diverse cultures of their students in order to better understand them. This active engagement can be gained through field experiences. Moreover, international study-abroad programs may help preservice teachers take into consideration the issues involved in the education system if they can see themselves as "global educators" (Malewski & Phillion, 2009). It is necessary for prospective teachers to explore countries around the world so that they become exposed to various cultures and ideologies. An understanding that can come from field experiences with diverse students and study-abroad experiences can help teachers gain a clearer understanding of the cultural background of students.

In addition to the teacher preparation described above, both preservice and in-service teachers need to be adequately prepared to work with immigrant students who are ELLs. Schoolwide professional development sessions that deal with pedagogy, assessment, and instruction related to ELLs can help in-service teachers learn more about teaching ELLs, in addition to teachers' attendance at conferences and other workshops (Sox, 2009). Furthermore, districts may offer workshops, such as basic courses on immigrant education, to non-ESL content-area teachers that cover ESL methodology for instruction and assessment, state and district policy on ESL, and management of electronic sources for ESL and peer training given by ESL teachers to non-ESL workmates (Wainer, 2004). As Sox (2009) pointed out, however, those kinds of professional development activities should be ongoing, with ESL personnel, other teachers, and administrators participating collaboratively. Although these suggestions sound overwhelming, the critical situation of teachers' lack of preparation for teaching ELLs requires teacher education programs to modify their curricula. A workable solution would be incorporating ELL content into a whole-teacher education program as discussed in Athanases and de Oliveira (2010). The framework provided and the teacher education program they studied can serve as guidance and an example for designing and implementing a programwide infusion of ELL issues according to content, process, and context.

In addition to addressing teacher preparation at the preservice and in-service levels, recruiting and retention of teachers are also worthy of attention. One of the major necessities is to hire multicultural teachers to help immigrant children settle into their new environment and to acquire a sense of belonging to the community (Cruickshank, 2004). In addition, it becomes vitally important to retain well-prepared teachers. Some 29% of teachers leave the profession after three years, and 39% leave after five years (Grant & Gillette, 2006).

The issues presented above all relate to social justice for immigrants. Immigrants need to have teachers who understand them as individuals with different cultural backgrounds and who are well prepared to meet their needs. Teacher education programs need to recruit and retain more multicultural teachers who can understand immigrants and help them adjust to a new environment, if they are newcomers to the country. Social justice for immigrants is closely connected to teacher education in the ways presented in this section. In the next section, we describe issues of immigrant education in Japan.

ISSUES OF IMMIGRANT EDUCATION IN JAPAN: A FOCUS ON BRAZILIAN IMMIGRANTS

Although more and more immigrants live in Japan, the Japanese educational system for immigrant students is not yet well established in many communities. Only a few schools, where numerous immigrant students attend, have prepared an individual curriculum for them (Aichi Prefecture, n.d.; Ikegami & Suenaga, 2010; Tamaki et al., 2009). Many immigrants have gone to Japan in search of better working conditions. These immigrants come from many places, such as China, South Korea, and Brazil. Brazilian immigrants are the third-largest immigrant population in Japan (Ministry of Justice, 2009), but they deserve special attention due to the current insufficient educational support for them.

In 1990, as a result of a governmental revision in Immigration Control and Refugee Recognition legislation in Japan, the number of immigrant guest workers, especially from Brazil, dramatically increased, as well as the number of their children (Aichi Prefecture, n.d.; Ikegami & Suenaga, 2010; Kumasaki, 2003; Terashima & Kawata, 2003; Yamanouchi, 2002). The Ministry of Justice (2009) reported that the number of immigrants from Brazil was 312,582, which accounts for 14.4% of the total number of immigrants currently residing in Japan. In addition, the Ministry of Education, Culture, Sports, Science and Technology (MEXT) reported that the number of students whose first language was Brazilian Portuguese and who needed proper Japanese instruction at school was 11,386 (MEXT, 2009). Only 30% of Brazilian students sufficiently understood Japanese, and only 10% of their schools prepared a special Japanese language curriculum for these students (Aichi Prefecture, n.d.; Tamaki et al., 2009).

There are two critical obstacles in the Japanese educational system in terms of social justice in teacher education: educational inequity (including achievement gaps) and language barriers. Additionally, these issues are closely related to cultural differences as well as lower instances of parental involvement in school events (Aichi Prefecture, n.d.; Ikegami & Suenaga; 2010; Kumasaki, 2003; Nakada & Muramatsu, 2006; Terashima & Kawata, 2003; Yamanouchi, 2002). In this section, the term "immigrant students" refers specifically to students from Brazil.

EDUCATIONAL INEQUITIES

Nowadays, many public schools in Japan are challenged by Brazilian students' high dropout rates and severely low attendance rates (Aichi Prefecture, n.d.; Tamaki et al., 2009; Terashima & Kawata, 2003). According to Terashima and Kawata (2003), about 23,000 Brazilian students (7–15 years old) did not attend school in 2000. One of the prominent obstacles to school attendance is the vast difference in cultural values between Japanese and Brazilian societies (Terashima & Kawata, 2003; Yamanouchi, 2002). As a result, many Brazilian students feel uncomfortable staying in class and tend to avoid school (Terashima & Kawata, 2003; Yamanouchi, 2002).

Terashima and Kawata (2003) mentioned that many Brazilian students experienced difficulties in Japanese and social studies classes, while they preferred physical education, art, and music. Besides adequate literacy, Japanese and social studies classes require basic knowledge of Japanese culture. Without sufficient literacy skills and cultural knowledge, immigrant students are hardly able to keep up with classes and gradually lose motivation. Consequently, there are widening educational gaps between the majority and minority students (Aichi Prefecture, n.d.; Kumasaki, 2003; Terashima & Kawata, 2003; Yamanouchi, 2002).

Teachers' insufficient knowledge and experiences of working with immigrant students aggravate these educational inequities (Kumasaki, 2003; Nakada & Muramatsu, 2006; Tamaki et al., 2009). Although many teachers are eager to work to help immigrant students, teachers face as many difficulties as minority students. The most prominent obstacles are a lack of understanding of the target culture and field experiences, as well as language barriers (Kumasaki, 2003: Tamaki et al., 2009; Terashima & Kawata, 2003). Many current teacher education programs are designed for Japanese students, and the evaluation criteria are not suitable for immigrant students (Nakada & Muramatsu, 2006; Tamaki et al., 2009). Preservice and in-service teachers need to learn to work with immigrant students and understand their students' culture in depth before they teach in class (Kumasaki, 2003; Nakada & Muramatsu, 2006; Tamaki et al., 2009).

Another prominent reason for the low attendance rate lies in students' domestic matters. Brazilian parents' expectations regarding school differ greatly from those of Japanese parents (Aichi Prefecture, n.d.; Terashima & Kawata, 2003; Yamanouchi, 2002). Many Brazilian parents come to Japan as guest workers; therefore, some parents, especially those who are not planning to stay long in Japan, seem to send their children to public schools as a daycare service because the public schools in Japan cost much less than the Brazilian private schools in Japan (Aichi Prefecture, n.d.; Terashima & Kawata, 2003; Yamanouchi, 2002). As a result, although many immigrant parents understand that academic success is significant, they become indifferent to their children's academic achievement because, as guest workers, their priorities are to work hard and earn money (Aichi Prefecture, n.d.; Kumasaki, 2003).

Kumasaki (2003) reported that many immigrant parents indicated that language barriers also remarkably prevented them from participating in class and school events. Terashima and Kawata (2003) insisted that, to reduce educational inequities, educators must consider how "Brazilian students who cannot speak Japanese" and "Japanese teachers who cannot speak Portuguese" could cooperate to establish an educational environment that would benefit all parties (p. 33). The following section considers the issue of language barriers.

Language Barriers

When immigrant children come to Japan, many of them need to learn Japanese to fully understand lessons (Aichi Prefecture, n.d.; Kumasaki, 2003; Nakada & Muramatsu, 2006). Language barriers can cause misunderstanding and conflict with teachers and classmates, strong anxiety and frustration, and lower motivation for studying (Ikegami & Suenaga, 2010; Kumasaki, 2003; Terashima & Kawata, 2003). These immigrant students need language support on a daily basis.

With some practical examples, many scholars advocate that teachers provide additional Japanese courses and supplemental lessons for immigrant students rather than compel them to only take the same courses with Japanese-majority students (Aichi Prefecture, n.d.; Ikegami & Suenaga, 2010; Kumasaki, 2003; Tamaki et al., 2009; Terashima & Kawata, 2003). Several public schools in the Aichi and Gunma regions, where a large number of

Brazilian students live, hire language instructors and native speakers of Portuguese, sometimes volunteer teachers, and provide Japanese classes to support students' typical coursework, such as Japanese, social studies, and math. The students can study at Saturday lessons, supplementary lessons, and after-school lessons with language aids (Aichi Prefecture, n.d.; Ikegami & Suenga, 2010). It is practical for students to receive education that goes beyond curriculum to adjust the situation appropriately, which is needed or suitable for immigrant students' demands (Cochran-Smith, 2004; Kumasaki, 2003; Tamaki et al., 2009).

Bilingual education is also advocated as an effective approach (Aichi Prefecture, n.d.; Ikegami & Suenaga, 2010; Tamaki et al., 2009). Bilingual teachers and volunteers can help immigrant students with learning as well as listen to their concerns. In fact, Ikegami and Suenaga (2010) reported that employing bilingual teachers in Gunma contributed to immigrant students' academic improvement, and as a result, the high school attendance rate for Brazilian students was improved. Although recruiting bilingual teachers in Portuguese and Japanese is an ideal solution, there are some issues in employment. It is not easy to secure certified Japanese teachers who can speak Portuguese because bilingual Japanese-Portuguese teachers are less common compared to bilingual Japanese-English teachers (Tamaki et al., 2009). On the other hand, it is also difficult to recruit native Portuguese speakers as teachers. For example, Ota-city, Gunma, required applicants to be certified in teaching at Brazilian universities and also qualified at the highest level of the Japanese Language Proficiency Test (JLPT) to become public school teachers (Nikkei Shinbun, 2004). This high threshold condition probably prevented candidates from applying.

The language barrier also causes parents to become less involved in school events. Many parents who do not understand Japanese cannot communicate with school teachers or read the school newsletter, which informs them of upcoming events. Consequently, these parents have few connections with schools (Kumasaki, 2003). Thus, many parents do not participate in school events because of insufficient Japanese language proficiency. Schools need to provide translators for the Brazilian parents to inform these parents of school rules or Japanese culture, as well as to create productive relationships (Kumasaki, 2003).

Teacher Preparation for Immigrant Students in Japan

We must face a considerable number of problems in providing sufficient education for immigrant students in Japan. To overcome these problems, a fundamental restructuring of teacher education programs is seriously needed in Japan. For example, underdeveloped programs at the university level aimed at educating teachers about how to handle students from minority backgrounds need considerable revision (Nakada & Muramatsu,

2006; Tamaki et al., 2009). Tamaki et al. (2009) mentioned that present teacher education programs make no allowances for high rates of immigrant student enrollment. Also, the current evaluation style, which places a high value on students' academic performance, should be reconsidered (Nakada & Muramatsu, 2006; Tamaki et al., 2009)

Nakada and Muramatsu (2006) pointed out that although several universities have many Japanese students who have attended school along with immigrant students, the teacher education programs at those schools do not always show a positive attitude toward reconstructing the curricular status quo. Nakada and Muramatsu (2006) emphasized that the Japanese students who once received education with Brazilian students are significantly motivated to teach immigrant students. Such students also have a more positive attitude toward learning with immigrant students with respect to cross-cultural understanding. For these reasons, they suggested that schools need to introduce more positive teacher training with regard to working with immigrant students.

Developing preservice teachers' language skills will be helpful in establishing trustful relationships and communicating with students and parents. Tamaki et al. (2009) stated that it would be ideal for preservice teachers to learn the target language before they work in the actual field. They also mentioned that teacher education programs should offer more language courses. However, they pointed out there are many difficulties in making this possible, such as the inefficiency of short-term lessons and difficulties employing native speakers at the university (Tamaki et al., 2009).

Employing native speakers and bilingual teachers is also considered an effective solution (Aichi Prefecture, n.d.; Tamaki et al., 2009; Terashima & Kawata, 2003). However, this ideal proposal is constrained by employment issues, as previously mentioned. Cochran-Smith (2004) claimed that teacher preparation presents a learning problem as well as a "political problem" (p. 2). It is disheartening to evaluate effective candidates who are willing to support students in the minority by their nationalities and the scores of high-stakes testing, such as JLPT. Zeichner (2009) and Cruickshank (2004) emphasized the importance of recruiting more teachers from minority groups. Likewise, Japanese teacher education programs should voluntarily accept a variety of people with exceptional conditions to provide more diverse teaching.

CONCLUSION

In this chapter, we examined several issues surrounding immigrant students and teacher education programs. We found quite a few similarities regarding educational issues between the United States and Japan, such as the language barriers and lack of teacher preparation for working with immigrant students. We ascertained that each country has particular problems that arise from their differentiated cultural conflicts, heterogeneity, and homogeneity. Our most prominent finding is that, regardless of whether the countries differ, each issue in both the United States and Japan is composed of a mixture of educational problems, and some issues are closely related not only to teachers and students but also to parents and community. Educators should tackle these multilayered problems with multidimensional perspectives rather than separate viewpoints. Particularly, three strategies should be prioritized in both countries. First, incorporating immigrants' culture into course content will help students feel that they belong in class because the curriculum also reflects their culture. In addition, teachers need to understand their students' culture in depth. Second, recruiting immigrant teachers will assist students to overcome their anxiety related to language and cultural barriers. Furthermore, immigrant teachers can serve as role models for students in their identity formation. Additionally, immigrant teachers may assist teachers from the majority groups to better help immigrant students and to understand multiple perspectives. Finally and most importantly, in-service and preservice teachers should be better prepared to teach immigrant students and to employ proper approaches in teaching immigrant students.

Although we referred to education systems in two different contexts, the U.S. and Japanese education systems, we think it is necessary for immigrant students to receive socially just education, because equal education is a right of every child regardless of ethnicity, language, or culture. In our viewpoint, teachers are central in promoting educational equality for immigrant students. Therefore, teacher education programs must equip all teachers with skills and dispositions to be able to teach students that are different in terms of cultural backgrounds to promote socially just education for all children. Teachers need to understand that "We" are the ones who can make a child's future brighter and better. Don't we think we as teachers need to be on the side of the child?

Authors' Note

The authors contributed equally to the preparation and writing of this chapter.

REFERENCES

Aichi Prefecture. (n.d.). *Brazil-jin no Kodomo no Kyouiku ni Kansuru Ichi-kousatsu*. Retrieved from www.geocities.jp/ronjiruchikara/tabunka.pdf

Athanases, S. Z., & de Oliveira, L. C. (2010). Toward program-wide coherence in preparing teachers to teach and advocate for English language learners. In T. Lucas (Ed.), *Teacher preparation for linguistically diverse classrooms: A resource for teacher educators* (pp. 195–215). New York, NY: Routledge.

Chu, S.Y. (2009). Implementation of supportive school programs for immigrant students in the United States. *Preventing School Failure, 53,* 67–72.

Cochran-Smith, M. (2003). Learning and unlearning: The education of a teacher educator. *Teaching and Teacher Education, 19,* 5–28.

Cochran-Smith, M. (2004). *Walking the road: Race, diversity, and social justice in teacher education.* New York, NY: Teachers College Press.

Cruickshank, K. (2004). Towards diversity in teacher education: Teacher preparation of immigrant teachers. *European Journal of Teacher Education, 27,* 125–138.

Davis, R. D., Ramahlo, T., Beyerbach, B., & London, A. P. (2008). A culturally relevant teaching course: Reflecting pre-service teachers' thinking. *Teaching Education, 19,* 223–234.

Garcia, E. (2005). *Teaching and learning in two languages: Bilingualism and schooling in the United States.* New York, NY: Teachers College Press.

Garcia, E., Arias, M. B., Harris Murri, N. J., & Serna, C. (2010). Developing responsive teachers: A challenge for a demographic reality. *Journal of Teacher Education, 61,* 132–142.

Grant, C. A., & Gillette, M. (2006). A candid talk to teacher educators about effectively preparing teachers who can teach everyone's children. *Journal of Teacher Education, 57,* 292–299.

Howard, G. R. (2007). As diversity grows, so must we. *Educational Leadership, 64,* 16–22.

Ikegami, M., & Suenaga, T. S. (2010). Gumma-ken Ota-shi ni Okeru Gaikokujin Jidou Seito ni Taisuru Nihongo Kyouiku no Genjyou to Kadai: Bilingual Kyouin no Yakuwari to Bogo ni yoru Shien wo Kangaeru. *Waseda Studies in Japanese Language Education, 4*(5), 1–13.

Kumasaki, S. (2003). Gaikoku-jin no Gimu-kyouiku Shugaku wo Meguru Shomondai: Brazil-jin Jidou/Seito no Baai. *Journal of International Student Center at Shinshu University, 4,* 139–150.

Levels, M., Dronkers, J., & Kraaykamp, G. (2008). Immigrant children's educational achievement in Western countries: Origin, destination, and community effects on mathematical performance. *American Sociological Review, 73,* 835–853.

Lucas, T., Villegas, A. M., & Freedson-Gonzalez, M. (2008). Linguistically responsive teacher education: Preparing classroom teachers to teach English language learners. *Journal of Teacher Education, 59,* 361–373.

Malewski, E., & Phillion, J. (2009). International field experiences: The impact of class, gender and race on the perceptions and experiences of preservice teachers. *Teaching and Teacher Education: An International Journal of Research and Studies, 25,* 52–60.

McDonald, M. & Zeichner, K. (2009). Social justice teacher education. In W. Ayers, T. Quinn, & D. Stovall (Eds.), *Handbook of social justice in education* (pp. 595–610). New York, NY: Routledge.

Ministry of Education, Culture, Sports, Science and Technology (MEXT). (2009). *Nihongo Shidou ga Hitsuyou na Gaikokujin Seito no Ukeire Jyoukyou-tou ni Kansuru Chousa (Heisei 20) no Kekka ni Tsuite.* Retrieved March 20, 2011, from http://www.mext.go.jp/b_menu/houdou/21/07/1279262.htm

Ministry of Justice. (2009). *Kokuseki-betsu Gaikokujin Tourokusha no Suii.* Retrieved from http://www.moj.go.jp/content/000049970.pdf

Nakada, T., & Muramatsu, M. (2006). Possibility of co-entering school for foreign and Japanese children: Analyzed from Japanese student's attitude survey concerning origin children. *Journal of Jissen Sougou Center at Aichi Kyouiku University, 10,* 69–78.

Nikkei Shinbun. (2004). *Nihongo Tannou na Birazil-jin Kyouin Boshu: Gaikoku-jin Kyouiku Tokubetsuku no Ota-shi.* Retrieved from http://www.nikkeyshimbun.com.br/2004/040721-73colonia.html

Oikonomidoy, E. (2011). Immigrant-responsive multicultural education in the United States. *Diaspora, Indigenous and Minority Education, 5,* 17–32. doi:10.1080/15595692.2011.534400

Solorzano, R. W. (2008). High stakes testing: Issues, implications, and remedies for English language learners. *Review of Educational Research, 78,* 260–329.

Sox, A. K. (2009). Latino immigrant students in Southern schools: What we know and still need to learn. *Theory Into Practice, 48*(4), 312–318. doi:10.1080/00405840903102912

Tamaki, M., Harada, M., & Wakabayashi, H. (2009). Kyouiku Jissen no Shiten kara Miru Gaikokujin Jidou-seito Kyouiku no Jenjyou to Kadai. *Journal of Faculty of International Studies Utsunomiya University, 27,* 135–153.

Terashima, T., & Kawata, M. (2003). Kokusai Rikai Kyouiku to Nikkei Brazil-jin no Kyouiku (2). *Jounal of the Department of Education at Gifu University, 52*(1), 1–34.

U.S. Census Bureau. (2011). *The 2011 statistical abstract.* Retrieved from http://www.census.gov/compendia/statab/2011edition.html

Vadivelu, V. M. (2007). Education system and teacher training in India and Ethiopia. *Ethiopian Journal of Education and Sciences, 3,* 97–102.

Valdes, G. (1998). The world outside and inside schools: Language and immigrant children. *Educational Researcher, 27*(6), 4–18.

Wainer, A. (2004). The new Latino South and the challenge to public education: Strategies for educators and policymakers in emerging immigrant communities. Retrieved March 27, 2011, from http://eric.ed.gov/PDFS/ED502060.pdf

Yamanouchi, Y. (2002). Gakkou ni Okeru Fubyoudou: Brazil-jim Marcia no Jirei kara. *Journal of Kyushu University, 5,* 207–221.

Zeichner, K. M. (2009). *Teacher education and the struggle social justice.* New York: Routledge.

CHAPTER 4

CHOCOLATE-COVERED TWINKIES

Social Justice and Superficial Aims in Teacher Education

Jubin Rahatzad, Jason Ware, and Mark Haugen

Many teacher education programs indeterminately incorporate the terms "transformative research" or "social justice" into their vision statements (Zeichner, 2009). However, the implied meanings of social justice often lack clarity, thus becoming nothing more than catchphrases. While teacher education programs have good intentions, not clarifying the meaning of social justice ignores oppressive realities. Furthermore, the demographic imperative (Zeichner, 2009) creates a rift of understanding between an increasingly diverse student population and a homogeneous teacher population (Cochran-Smith, 2004). Therefore, strategically placing the terms transformative or social justice within teacher education programs superficially acknowledges the demographic imperative without committing to true praxis for equity. For this reason, we posit that teacher education programs need to be explicit about why and how they conceptualize notions of transformative social justice in the vision statements that provide the philos-

Teacher Education for Social Justice: Perspectives and Lessons Learned, pages 35–52.
Copyright © 2013 by Information Age Publishing

ophy behind their programs. Our assertion recognizes the good intentions behind the frequent use of transformative and/or social justice, but takes issue with the vagueness that often ensues in envisioning an alternative future. This is important because teacher education plays an integral part in changing the purpose of education from social reproduction to revolutionary dynamism (McLaren, 2007).

We connect theory to concrete examples, delineating the institutional and structural racism within schooling (Ladson-Billings & Tate, 1995) in order to elaborate on the necessity for teacher education to resist it and work toward social justice. Additionally, we provide a transformative social justice vision for teacher education programs based on the analysis of a representative example of superficiality from an R-1 Midwestern University. The vision proposed is transformative in that it will enhance preservice teachers' joint theoretical and practical considerations of social justice. First, we will discuss our conceptualization of teacher education for social justice, which, as Zeichner (2009) points out, "see[s] schooling and teacher education as crucial elements in the making of a more just society" (p. 16). The process toward a more just society will be based in Freire's (2010) conceptualizations around pedagogical intent. Then an alternative vision for teacher education, based in Freirean pedagogy, is proposed in order to work toward a more just society.

As Darling-Hammond (2010, p. 35) argues, "Colleges of teacher education have a major responsibility for which path the nation travels" (p. 35). How education is conceptualized carries many implications with it. Therefore, in an open society, the definition of education should be a continuous process that is widely debated. Furthermore, any goals critical of the dominant system that become co-opted by the same system must be revealed as artificial and compromised.

The following poem was written in the Faubourg Marigny neighborhood in New Orleans, Louisiana, by a sidewalk poet who writes commissioned poems on a typewriter. The authors requested he write a poem about them and gave him a brief description of them along with a chapter synopsis. What emerged was awareness of the openness of possibilities and opportunities that are available throughout life experiences, especially encounters with difference. This is what was created:

Multicultural promotion without self-ownership
is like slavery before we knew it was bad

but tell this to the teacher with the chocolate-covered twinkie in her hand
and she might say "we always knew" or "isn't that sad"
but the truth of the matter is that all this is rad

take a black man, an Iranian (brown but whitewashed spongecake),

and a real life whitey
and you get the best educational chapter (no joke) you ever had

eat that twinkie up fellows (Joshua Willis, 2011)

CONCEPTUALIZING SOCIAL
JUSTICE WITHIN TEACHER EDUCATION

One primary goal for a social justice-focused teacher education program should be dialogically engaging preservice teachers' self-awareness. Here, dialogically represents two or more divergent perspectives interacting and converging to create shared knowledge and transcending dialogue as a technique (Freire, 2010). So, more than teacher educators conversing with preservice teachers in a back-and-forth rhythm, dialogic activity gives credence to the social and political "character of the process of knowing," and is thus itself a "way of knowing" (Freire, 2010, p. 17). In creating this shared knowledge, it is imperative that preservice teachers acknowledge the nonneutral and political nature of institutionalized education as part of the process of *conscientização*, which, according to Freire (2010), refers to increasing one's critical consciousness related to the interplay of social, political, and economic contradictions. *Conscientização* inspires action against oppressive social, political, and economic realities (Freire, 2010). Dialogically engaging preservice teachers' self-awareness or *conscientização*, then, is to facilitate recognition of their complicity, by times, in oppressing students. This process creates shared knowledge about the oppressive reality in the demands of dominant culture assimilation that takes place in U.S. classrooms.

Culturally Responsive Teaching (CRT) is a concept that consistently comes up when we address social justice within teacher education (Cochran-Smith, 2004, Villegas & Lucas, 2002; Zeichner, 2009). CRT combines sociocultural consciousness, viewing the diverse backgrounds of students as resources for learning, as well as understanding and promoting knowledge creation from all students. Critical sociocultural consciousness can be developed through extensive collaboration with practitioners working "against the grain" (Cochran-Smith, 2004) with diverse populations, the incorporation of English as a second language (ESL) teaching strategies, and the study and incorporation of successful culturally responsive teaching strategies. CRT is a socially just teaching method in which learning opportunities for students are addressed (Chubbuck, 2010; Milner, 2010). The gaps in opportunity that exist for various learners explain much of the complaints generated by the largely ignorant concept of achievement gaps. There is no reason to think that all learners will meet any standard when the opportunities present for learners are stratified (Milner, 2010).

Increasing opportunities for learners will require, as one aspect, increasing opportunities for prospective teachers.

Although many CRT strategies can be learned, they do not negate the importance of recruiting teachers with diverse cultural backgrounds and social justice-oriented dispositions. Scholars (e.g., Cochran-Smith, 2004; McDonald & Zeichner, 2009; Zeichner, 2009) consistently address the demographic imperative, which refers to the increasing cultural, linguistic, racial, and socioeconomic divide between our nation's teachers and students as well as the differential access to educational opportunities by these groups. While educational systems in the United States systematically fail many students from varying cultural, racial, and socioeconomic backgrounds, so do U.S. teacher education programs in failing to recruit and engage teacher candidates from diverse backgrounds. Transformation of schools of education must consist of recruiting and admitting more teachers of ethnic/racial minorities to bridge the cultural gap between our teachers and students.

In addition, social justice must look beyond the school context to transform oppressive structures that perpetuate injustices (McLaren, 2007). Injustices such as differential access to educational opportunity, racism, sexism, classism, capitalism, pollution, and so on are maintained by our cultural capitalism and must be analyzed and critiqued. As the culture of power shifts away from anything resembling social justice, it perpetuates injustice through education that does not foster students' critical consciousness. Professors, preservice teachers, teachers, and students must be exposed to theoretical frameworks that provide the language to critique social structures. The process of social justice must name, be dialogically critical of, and praxis-oriented toward structures and policies that sustain injustice and limit our ability to seek humanization (Freire, 2010). Constant dialogue as pedagogy sustains transformative education, moving beyond rhetorical false charity found in strategic plans. It constructs knowledge that recognizes social injustice and creates a need to sustain relationships between what we do in the classroom and our effort to build a better society (McLaren, 2007). This pedagogy presupposes that *seres humanos*[1] main vocation is to act upon and transform their world, understanding the interrelationships of power, politics, culture, and history within the educational process.

Teacher education programs should reinforce preservice teachers' capacity to join with students in navigating and negotiating demands of dominant culture. Preservice teachers will have a base about how to dialogically engage future students in ways similar to how they were engaged within their respective teacher education programs. Dialogue as a joint effort

---

[1] Spanish for *human beings*. The use of Spanish or any other language is one tangible form of broadening what it means to be a teacher and teacher educator at any level and for any time and space.

should enhance both teacher and students' humanity through facilitating agency to impact and create knowledge and value systems. The humanization of shared knowledge creation is important because the process must resemble the envisioned future. This aspect of Freirean pedagogy, while mindful of contradictions throughout the process, is succinctly stated by Paul Goodman (Holt, 1970):

> Suppose you had the revolution you are talking and dreaming about. Suppose your side won, and you had the kind of society you wanted. How would you live, you personally, in that society? Start living that way now! Whatever you would do then, do it now. (p. 302)

Additional reflection upon the term social justice leads to another notion. Social justice is about equity through solidarity. With a bit more consideration, the conception of social justice is broadened and moves— perpetual movement—to a problematization of oppressive ideologies and politics. Teacher education for social justice, then, prepares teachers to create the pedagogical conditions in which problematizing dialogue can take place. However, a key question is what should be problematized?

OTHERNESS AND CONSTRUCTION OF THE CHOCOLATE-COVERED TWINKIE

Acknowledging and transforming a culture of difference that "others" people is at the core of teacher education for social justice. A culture of difference represents beliefs and social relations informed by magnifying human difference in ways that influence the disparate treatment of certain people. This creates "others" in contrast to the whitestream norm in the United States (Denis, 1997; Grande, 2004). Whitestream represents the standard of lived experience defined by White Anglo-Europeans (for the most part, although many Western Europeans have become part of the whitestream) and the construction of U.S. society based on this White experience. The Other represents those whose lived experience is different than or is in contrast to the whitestream. A culture of difference is perpetuated as a result of contemporary U.S. social relations defined by dominance of the object by the subject and obsequiousness on the part of the Other (produced by the whitestream).

The work of philosophers such as Hegel (1977) and Sartre (1943) theoretically underpins the term the "other." Their perspectives give way to understanding one's self-consciousness as a phenomenological function mediated through contact with others. In coming in contact with others, or those in whom people recognize few shared personal characteristics, be they physical traits, language use or cultural background, people become aware of how different they are from the other. In interacting with or experiencing the other, people become aware of how they perceive the other and how they are perceived by the other, which partially constructs people's self-consciousness. In this dynamic, an individual is both subject in perceiving and object in being perceived. Therefore, upon initial contact, both sides exemplify the possibility of object and subject. The process of othering, then, is mediated through structural and systemic power differentials that give rise to one side objectifying the other with little or no chance of being objectified itself in a similar manner; objectifying being critical in this process as it translates to controlling others' political, social and economic place and transcends the material to control one's psyche. In other words, othering results in the subjects' perception of the other as excessively different and therefore lacking, to become the basis for dehumanizing the other.

Throughout history, certain groups of people have had more political, social, and economic power than others; consider the notion of whitestream. The historicized possession and wielding of power distinguishes one side as the object of the other side (subject). Historical circumstances—physical and epistemological—influence initial encounters and thus highlight differences based on imbalances of social clout. How these imbalances are systemically justified and normalized leads to objectification. Hegel (1977) explains,

> This has a twofold significance: first, it has lost itself, for it finds itself as an *other* being; secondly, in doing so it has superseded the other, for it does not see the other as an essential being, but in the other sees its own self. It must supersede this otherness of itself. This is the supersession of the first ambiguity, and is therefore itself a second ambiguity. First, it must proceed to supersede the *other* independent being in order thereby to become certain of *itself* as the essential being. (p. 111, emphasis in original)

This ontology affirms the reinforcing nature of whitestream U.S. society. The constant Othering of all perceived to be outside of the whitestream coalesces with Freire's (2010) notion that the oppressed internalize characteristics of the oppressor, but also that the oppressor oppresses itself. Philosophical conceptualizations of the other unveil how the process of othering constrains the subject and the object. However, the subject possesses power as a privilege of geography, race, gender, and class, exercising its power over the Other.

Whitestream society has relegated parts of society, via the process of othering, to a lower status based on various social identities. These Others have in effect been cast aside, like a disregarded item, by the whitestream. For example, differences pronounced through language, cultural ideologies, and cultural expression have been systematically essentialized and superseded by whitestream culture. Said (2003) describes how Others are essentialized, in this case by the whitestream:

> It shares with magic and with mythology the self-containing, self-reinforcing character of a closed system, in which objects are what they are *because* they are what they are, for once, for all time, for ontological reasons that no empirical material can either dislodge or alter. (p. 70, emphasis in original)

Prominent historical cases within the U.S. context are the dispossession of Native Americans and the involuntary immigration of Africans for the purpose of slavery. Native Americans have largely been trapped in time from the whitestream perception (Grande, 2004), and have been historically subjected to an educational process that served the purpose of genocide (Adams, 1995). African Americans have not only been subjected by systems of slavery but a continuation of Jim Crow discrimination despite whitestream claims that the Jim Crow era ended with the 1960s Civil Rights Movement. Alexander (2010) reveals mass incarceration in the United States as a post–Civil Rights version of Jim Crow that African Americans (and Latinos) are subjected to in order to maintain whitestream control. More recently, the heightened rhetoric surrounding Middle Eastern Americans provides another example of how the whitestream Others its subjects. Tehranian (2009) asserts that Middle Easterners have not only been discriminated against in the United States but have been made invisible as well. The legal classification of Middle Easterners as "White" by the U.S. government ignores millions of Middle Eastern Americans' daily experience as "non-White." How the whitestream others those it objectifies has a variety of forms, but the important point here is that the whitestream others by exerting power and creating a culture of difference throughout the educational systems in the United States, including teacher education programs.

Through such an exertion of power, the whitestream oppresses those othered and limits the possibility of options for the future. Limitation of possibility maintains the prejudices and values that preservice teachers hold. Teacher education programs should not maintain these prejudices and values, but rather overturn the familiar for a critical analysis of society. As Zeichner (2009) points out, "Our government spends roughly 290 times more on defense research than it spends on research on education, and pours billions of dollars annually into the support of such things as weapons systems and tax relief for the rich" (p. 145). The normalization of such societal priorities reinforces and furthers the power of the whitestream and its ability to control social relations. Teacher education programs should be part of the resistance against such whitestream priorities that hurt all, including the whitestream in the long term. Teacher education programs should be spaces in which alternatives to the whitestream are developed.

TRANSFORMING TEACHER EDUCATION

With the broadening of considered possibilities in mind, we suggest that U.S. teacher education programs redefine the philosophical outlook. A representative teacher education program at an R-1 Midwestern University will be used an example for all teacher education programs that purport to advocate social responsibility, in this case based upon a mission of "transformative research." Such assertions outline the philosophy of a teacher education program. However, missions claiming to be socially just and/ or equitable are often gratuitous. For example, focusing on content without an integration of diversity issues across a teacher education program signifies that very little attention is paid to issues of diversity in education. Compartmentalizing diversity to a single multiculturalism class is evidence that a program does not take the demographic imperative seriously. This compartmentalization is symptomatic of educational policy at the state and federal levels (e.g., an obsessive insistence on corporatized high-stakes testing).

The first point this R-1 Midwestern University's teacher education program makes in its vision is that it will have global influence in responsive educational discovery and pedagogy. It goes on to proclaim that it will achieve excellence through several means. The first of these means is through transformative research; however, the program does not explain the meaning of "transformative research" anywhere in the mission, vision, or program structure. Although transformative research sounds admirable and words such as *excellence, exemplary,* and *impactful* are appealing, clear articulation of what the teacher education program aims to achieve is needed.

The mission of the aforementioned teacher education program focuses on what it purports to accomplish. The three objectives of the mission are (a) to propel scientific research about learning and human development, (b) to produce model educators and intellectuals with widespread influence, and (c) to provide for optimum educational achievement through teaching, research, and engagement. In order to accomplish these objectives, the teacher education program commits to several action items. The first of these is creating a culture of discovery or research. Additionally, the program commits to providing a responsive curriculum focused on preparing professional educators by empowering faculty, staff, and students to enhance positive change in highly diverse societies. Presumably, U.S. society is implicated by this assertion, yet providing a single course that addresses diversity issues is hardly a commitment to preparing future educators for a diverse society. In addition, the program supports interdisciplinary collaboration in order to work with critical educational issues and to better inform educational policy and programs. Such support of interdisciplinary collaboration is lacking when talking to faculty of specific subject areas within the teacher education program. Milner (2010) cites the example of a teacher who realized that knowing your science and teaching it was not sufficient in a racially diverse school. There is much cultural and social work to be done on the part of the teacher in order to relate the content to various students. Many teacher education programs do not prepare teachers for this aspect of the teaching profession.

The structure and assertions of this particular teacher education program continue to claim transformative research and social justice as integral parts. Although several disciplinary areas including but not limited to elementary, social studies, science, and art education are offered, there is a common mode of organization or structure running through them all. Most disciplines have major or area core requirements. However, the common thread running through each of the disciplinary areas within the teacher education program is the initial component. Within this phase of the program, preservice teachers are required to take two courses that introduce them to teaching as a career and issues of multiculturalism and education. These courses represent the teacher education program's approach to preparing preservice teachers to enact positive change within diverse communities. Within the course focused on multiculturalism and education, students are encouraged to consider a multitude of cultures, the majority of which are Others for the predominantly White, middle-class (and female at the elementary level) cohort of preservice teachers. Examples of such cultures include racial minorities, immigrants, queer identities within gender and sexuality, among others. While an introduction to Others is essential, teacher education programs must go beyond solely acknowledging their existence for a week in a single semester course. In order to truly enact positive change, critical dialogue regarding social justice must be interwoven into all courses and not relegated to introductory discussions about diversity.

The strategic plan of the College of Education at the R-1 Midwestern University states as part of its mission that it "prepares exceptional teachers." Also, it claims to "Attract and retain stellar, diverse faculty, staff and students." Part of its "Values and Culture" is "Multiculturalism," without any further description or explanation. Under the "goal" to "Model the inclusiveness of diverse ideas, cultures, and people," it states that the teacher education program aims to "Recruit, support, and retain a teacher education student population that reflects the diversity of the state and diversifies the teaching profession in [the particular state]." Furthermore, the claim is made that the College of Education works to ensure that the faculty represent the diversity of the nation. A critical analysis of this mission must question the purpose behind inclusivity if deep analysis is to occur. Is diversity promoted within this university's teacher education program for the sake of diversity without any thought to why the promotion of diversity might be beneficial? Even the urban field experience offered involves a couple of days of "immersion" in an urban setting but does not ask why it might be beneficial to immerse preservice teachers in possibly unfamiliar settings, or at least different from the whitestream. Even if there is a presence of "ethnic, gender, [and] international" diversity, will the stratified nature of U.S. society be questioned at its root?

The goal of inclusivity claims to provide courses related to globalization, multiculturalism, and/or diversity. Are these individually distinct topics? What is meant by globalization? What is meant by multiculturalism? All of this is unclear. On the "Diversity" page of this university's teacher education program's website, there are four total courses listed under Diversity Related Courses in Teacher Education (College of Education, 2009). Two of these courses are the introductory courses mentioned above. One of us is an instructor for one of these two introductory courses that are categorized as being related to "diversity." From this author's experience, it is blatantly evident that preservice teachers at the initial stage of their program have a hollow grasp of social relations. Most beginning preservice teachers struggle with macro-analysis of social relations and doubt the relevance of analyzing societal norms for the purpose of becoming a teacher. Thus, if this university's teacher education program aims to be transformative in nature, it must go beyond two courses that present diversity and move toward courses that critically analyze the aforementioned topics or it will simply continue to reinforce the status quo. Cochran-Smith (2004) recognizes this problem and states that "the intentions of programs are not necessarily implemented, particularly in the interactions of students and their supervisors and in methods and fieldwork courses" (p. 26).

Therefore, if this teacher education program does not initiate critical reflection for the majority of beginning students, then not much can be expected from the methods and fieldwork courses that follow wherein systemic analysis is often absent. It is questionable if this teacher education program has a chocolate covering or even a golden cake that covers the true nature of its white creamy filling. The whitestream rarely comes under the microscope for analysis and the status quo remains largely unquestioned.

When these preservice teachers graduate and enter the teaching workforce, their ability to analyze the local context of the community in which they teach is at best limited. Forced to "learn on the job," dysfunctional coping mechanisms develop and expectations for students are often lowered. Othering continues to dominate the ideological lens of the primarily whitestream teaching workforce. If students present problems for the teacher as a result of a culture of difference, then the teacher will often blame the problems on students' identities. Such dysfunctional coping mechanisms are partially the result of twinkie-like teacher education programs. Teacher education programs cannot be solely blamed for such an outcome; however, teacher education programs do, whether they choose to acknowledge it or not, play a part in the social reproductive nature of the current educational system (Apple, 2001). Therefore, teacher educators should reflect and engage in their asserted goals to create a more just society. The whitestream should be challenged by teacher education programs. *Tenemos que desafiar privilegio en cualquier de sus formas. Hay que saber alternativas para el bienestar del futuro.*[2] As Zeichner (2009) asserts,

> While we must not romanticize and delude ourselves about how much we can accomplish with changes to the teacher education curriculum within existing structures, we also must not exhibit moral cowardice and back off from the task of preparing teachers to be advocates for social justice for all children. (p. 56)

Teacher education programs should pay attention to the words used in their mission statements. Using terms like *social responsibility*, *multiculturalism*, and *diversity* in vague and undefined manners is problematic. What social responsibility looks like and how it incorporates diversity inherent in multiculturalism is often not well articulated. Lacking clarity in meaning and purpose signifies the noncommittal nature of a program toward social justice. What is meant by social justice and equity needs to be explicitly defined and then put into practice through major changes to many teacher education programs.

SOCIALLY JUST TEACHER EDUCATION

A teacher education framework that focuses on social justice must be reconceptualized in order to be genuine and effective. We propose four concrete changes that embody a commitment to a socially just teacher education program. The first change is to create university campus spaces within local public schools. Second, in order for a more social justice-oriented teacher education program, we propose critical engagement of educational policy as a central theme, engagement that works tensions between the existing social order and alternate world views. Third, we propose requiring second-language proficiency and an immersive study-abroad experience. Finally, we propose an admissions process that holistically assesses prospective teachers in order to diversify the field of teacher candidates.

Physical Campus Space

For true transformation of teacher education programs, we propose greater connection between colleges of education and local schools and communities through college of education campuses at local high schools

---

[2] Spanish for, "We must challenge privilege in all its forms. Alternatives must be learned for future well-being."

serving the most diverse population in the respective areas. Physical college of education spaces within local public high schools will facilitate increased collaboration, inquiry, as well as knowledge exchange and creation between practitioners, academics, preservice teachers, and students. Creating university campus spaces within local public schools will enhance collaborative opportunities and dialogic activity, which is a critical piece in taking action against social, political, and economic oppression. The purpose, then, in having university spaces within public schools is to place these key individuals in concert with each other to enhance both awareness of and action against systemic educational oppression.

Researchers and teacher educators, in part, focus on illuminating modes of instruction in the classroom, and beyond that, create optimal educational outcomes. Understanding the oppressive nature of school and community structures is imperative, but having all voices articulating what "optimal outcomes" look like and what they are in the face of oppression is of utmost importance. Researchers often deal with educational theories to inform particular praxis, while preservice teachers are on the ground or in the "real world" operating within classroom constraints imposed by school administrators. We imagine university spaces within public schools that will dismantle the walls separating what happens at universities from what goes on in the schools.

The current relations between university teacher education programs and public schools may be a result of constraints placed on increased dialogue. Financial issues may be one factor. This speaks to the market-obsessed ideology that seeks to reduce public funds in order to concentrate wealth in the hands of the few. Again, the field and practice of education at-large can be influential in changing the perception that public funds are inefficient or controlled by a supposed "bogey-man," as the state apparatus is often painted to be. Harkening back to Horace Mann and Thomas Jefferson's visions of what a successful nation entails, a free public education for all was integral to the development and maintenance of such a nation. This is not a new or drastic idea, but rather one of pursuing equity for all. Another constraint may be the time (or lack thereof) of teacher educators and practicing teachers. In a corporatized educational system, time is controlled obsessively, and routines are seen as ends within themselves. Sight of the larger issues may be clouded or forgotten, but it is for this reason that teacher preparation must engage candidates in critical thought about the profession itself. The supposed "gap" between theory and practice is self-imposed and ideological in nature. There is no reason for teachers to not be intellectual actors and for teacher educators to be actively engaged actors. Freire's praxis embodied in *conscientização* marries the world of ideas and the world of action. One is incomplete without the other if the goal is to work toward a more just society (Freire, 2010).

We suggest that what goes on within universities and public schools should not be drastically different. Research universities focus on research and discovery, while smaller universities and colleges focus more on classroom instruction. Public schools are a perfect site for action research by preservice teachers and for research in general by university researchers and teacher educators. University spaces within public schools provide ease of movement and invite perpetual exchange between the two spaces. As Cochran-Smith (2004) notes, "Inquiry is most effective within a larger culture of collaboration where novices and experienced professionals alike learn from, interpret, and ultimately alter the day-to-day life of schools" (p. 27).

Critical Engagement

As educational stakeholders, that is, students, preservice teachers, teachers, and teacher educators, increasingly collaborate and become conscious of the complicit (or noncomplicit) role they play in supporting the current capitalistic structure of education (i.e., reliance on standardized tests), they must also have access to a pedagogical framework to critique and transform the system. Our vision interweaves critical engagement of educational policy, whitestream ideals, and capitalistic notions throughout preservice teachers' coursework, allowing problematization of dominant policies and empowering teachers and students as change agents within education and society at-large. We believe that in order for a teacher education program to truly embody a social justice orientation, preservice teachers must view themselves as active agents and understand that social change begins with critical engagement.

Critical engagement obligates preservice teachers to think about the social and political ways in which their work is embedded. This can begin through inquiry. As Zeichner (2009) suggests, participatory action research can be a form of inquiry within the local educational context that engages educational stakeholders in efforts to improve education. Participatory action research allows researchers to be agents in their own education and is one way to create culturally responsive teachers. However, as Zeichner warns,

> It is important not to romanticize what can be accomplished by action research or any other teaching strategy that is used in pre-service teacher education. Action research is not a panacea for the sorry state of U.S. teacher education with regard to issues of equity and diversity. (p. 64)

It is important to note that action research is not inherently linked to social justice. Preservice teachers doing action research in our program should orient their work toward a more thorough understanding of students from diverse backgrounds and how educational structures work to maintain whitestream dominance.

Second-Language Proficiency and Study Abroad

As students enter teacher education programs, many are unaware of contemporary power relations on the basis of race, class, gender, sexuality, religion, and other social identities. In particular, preservice teachers of White, monolingual, middle-class backgrounds have not experienced being "othered" in U.S. society. Consequently, we propose a required, immersive, and extensive study-abroad experience. Study-abroad experiences are effective when preservice teachers are in an environment with people and language(s) completely different from their own. Immersive means more than a couple months (and definitely more than the couple of weeks that many programs constitute) in another country and necessitates living with a local host family while abroad. Phillion et al. (2008) highlight how brief and "safe" study-abroad experiences can often reinforce the pitfalls of White privilege. Students who spend a month abroad may develop notions of pity for the Others with whom they interact. Also, the perception of superiority for White, monolingual, middle-class *estadounidenses*[3] can become further entrenched with brief contact with cultural Others that always includes a safe "out" if necessary.

Instead, preservice teachers should be made to feel uncomfortable and more importantly forced to deal with discomfort. This experience then should be equated to how their social identities may make Others feel this way in the United States and all over the world. While it is true that the intersections of social identities create complex situations in which many people may be both privileged and Othered simultaneously, White preservice teachers should indulge in being the complete Other. Then dialogue can ensue about the complexities. Until most preservice teachers have experienced being forced to be the Other and develop genuine empathy (among other sentiments), then a true understanding of working with Others is not possible.

The majority of teacher education programs absolutely fails on creating such experiences. Study-abroad programs that are less than 6 months in duration will usually be unsuccessful at creating the experience of Other. Preservice teachers should realize what it feels like to invest emotionally in a place where they are not the norm. The authors recommend a minimal 9-month period (one academic year) required for all preservice teach-

---

[3] Spanish for American. A better translation would be "United Statian," since *American* in Spanish can mean a person from the Americas. This aspect of the English language and how it is used in the United States imperially places United Statians above all other peoples of the Americas. This is another example of tangible altering mindsets.

ers. This may seem bold to some, but readers should ask themselves why *estadounidenses* often reject forced exposure to places outside the United States. The cultural isolation of the United States that lends to notions of cultural superiority should be ruptured. When compromises are made on this issue, then teacher education programs fail to provide well-rounded future teachers.

Study-abroad experiences for preservice teachers should also complement foundational coursework in a second language or preexisting second-language abilities. Therefore, in the United States, all preservice teachers will know English and at least one other language. In the contemporary context, Spanish, Cantonese, Mandarin, or Arabic are a few examples of useful second languages if a preservice teacher plans to teach in the United States. When a study-abroad experience aids language acquisition, then the preservice teacher is being prepared to teach more students. Such a strategy for language proficiency enables teacher education programs to prepare all teachers to teach more students (Milner, 2010; Zeichner, 2009).

Of course, for strategies to be discussed about second-language requirements within teacher education, it is necessary for programs to develop philosophies that are serious about preparing teachers to teach all students. The United States has always been and is a dynamic environment for language. The imperialist-based idea that English is the dominant language of the world is prejudiced in its origins. While English is an important global language, there are also other important global languages. In order for the United States to be actively engaged in a global context, it is necessary for its teachers to be prepared. Being proficient in more than one language not only aids teachers in teaching English language learners, but it also allows a teacher or any person to analyze and view the world through multiple theoretical lenses. If students are taught by globally aware teachers, then greater opportunities will exist. In addition, as global dynamics change, it would benefit the United States to have a group of critical thinkers—its teachers—to help adjust to new global realities. Such proposals are not "pie-in-the-sky" ideas but rather practical. Teacher preparation should move beyond "cuddly" acknowledgments of multiculturalism and engage within other cultures, such as language and geographic location. A required second-language proficiency and immersive study-abroad experience are needed for all teacher education programs. Such a requirement would also attract a more diverse group of teacher candidates, specifically those willing to experience other cultures directly and not simply experience the world through prepackaged cultural curriculum.

Holistic Admissions

Addressing the cultural divide between teachers and students is an important element in creating a more just teacher education program. We propose an admissions process that holistically assesses disposition, experience, and life change. As Freire (2010) points out, educators must be attuned to the structural conditions in which their students live in order to communicate effectively. Such an admissions process would value cultural funds of knowledge (Moll, 1992), dispositions that relate to social justice, and students from and with positive dispositions to diverse cultural backgrounds.

The larger question that applies to teacher recruitment is *what knowledge is of most worth and why?* Grant & Sleeter (2007) provide an example of what teachers should be aware of within their society. The fact is that knowledge is constructed and created while some people and communities have greater influence in the process of knowledge construction. Power dynamics related to socioeconomic class and other social identities determines whether or not the cultural background of a given student is actively valued in the schooling process. Valenzuela (1999) has shown what happens when a student's background is not valued by educators and that for an educational process to be authentic it cannot be subtractive. Subtracting a student's cultural background, through various means such as ignoring and/or marginalizing, dehumanizes the whole learning process. For a more humanistic learning process, it is necessary to explore, learn, acknowledge, and actively value a student's cultural background. No student, for whatever reason, should feel that the divide between home and school is too vast to connect. Schooling should not be to promote a predetermined superior culture; instead the purpose of schooling is meant to equip the student with and explore the tools within whitestream (Grande, 2004) culture and within a student's culture. Using the iceberg analogy of culture can be useful for preservice teachers in understanding that what is visible (10% of the iceberg) is a minor part of a person's background. Building relationships with students allows teachers to learn about the other 90% of a student's culture (Grant & Sleeter 2007).

Admissions processes and requirements for teacher education programs should rigorously analyze the disposition of prospective preservice teachers. Interviews and written statements can ask specific questions about how applicants feel about potential future groups of students. Also, it may be productive to have teacher education courses in conjunction with a required major in another field. The perspectives that biologists or political scientists can bring to teacher education can create unique blends of insights about what schooling is and should be in the United States. Alternatives should be explored, and teacher education programs should provide space for preservice teachers to engage in knowledge construction about what education and learning should be about as opposed to what they are currently about. There are always risks involved with learning, but attempting to control the learning process, especially through biased standardization and simplification of knowledge, is detrimental to society as a whole. Acknowledging the constructive aspect of knowledge is a start for admissions standards. This way teacher education programs can help ensure that critical thinkers enter their programs.

THE CHOCOLATE-COVERED TWINKIE

Teacher education needs to be self-reflective and critical in order to engage in the genuine work of creating a more just society. Thus, enhancing the potential for programs with clear and intentional social justice visions is necessary. Alternatives to hegemonic whitestream systems should be considered and embraced in order to close the opportunity gap. Human beings are dynamically unique individuals; imposing a singular approach to social relations upon all *seres humanos* is a practice in futility. Therefore, teacher education programs should embrace a diverse society and be clear and explicit in their philosophies, instead of using mission statements as public relations documents. Programs must be constructed in order to prepare all teachers to teach all students if social equity is the goal. The chocolate covering and golden-brown cake must be more than covers for the creamy white filling. Whiteness and the hegemonic whitestream must be addressed directly if teacher education is to be against oppressive systems. New ways of thinking and new possibilities cannot be discarded because there is no tangible vision that can be justified by the dominant system. Self-enclosed and isolated systems will not be prosperous in the future; a broadening of what education means is necessary. Alcoff (2007) warns against such isolated systems that breed epistemological ignorance. Teachers and teacher educators should be aware of more than their immediate environment.

REFERENCES

Adams, D. W. (1995). *Education for extinction: American Indians and the boarding school experience, 1875–1928.* Lawrence: University Press of Kansas.

Alcoff, L. M. (2007). Epistemologies of ignorance: Three types. In S. Sullivan & N. Tuana (Eds.), *Race and epistemologies of ignorance* (pp. 39–57). Albany: State University of New York Press.

Alexander, M. (2010). *The new Jim Crow: Mass incarceration in the age of colorblindness.* New York, NY: New Press.

Apple, M. (2001). Markets, standards, teaching, and teacher education. *Journal of Teacher Education, 52*(3), 182–195.

Chubbuck, S. M. (2010). Individual and structural orientations in socially just teaching: Conceptualization, implementation, and collaborative work. *Journal of Teacher Education, 61*(3), 197–210.

Cochran-Smith, M. (2004). *Walking the road: Race, diversity, and social justice in teacher education.* New York, NY: Teachers College Press.

College of Education, Purdue University, (2009). *Strategic Plan: 2009–2014.* Retrieved from http://education.purdue.edu/about_us/strategic_plan/index.html:

Darling-Hammond, L. (2010). Teacher education and the American future. *Journal of Teacher Education, 6*(1–2), 35–47.

Denis, C. (1997). *We are not you: First nations and Canadian modernity.* Toronto, Canada: University of Toronto Press.

Freire, P. (2010). *Pedagogy of the oppressed.* New York, NY: Continuum.

Grande, S. (2004). *Red pedagogy: Native American social and political thought.* Lanham, MD: Rowman & Littlefield.

Grant, C. A., & Sleeter, C. E. (2007). *Doing multicultural education for achievement and equity.* New York, NY: Routledge.

Hegel, G. W. F. (1977). *Hegel's phenomenology of spirit* (J. N. Findlay, Trans.). Oxford, UK: Oxford University Press. (Original work published 1952)

Holt, J. (1970). *What do I do Monday?* New York, NY: Dell.

Ladson-Billings, G., & Tate, W. F. (1995). Toward a critical race theory of education. *Teachers College Record, 97,* 47–68.

McDonald, M., & Zeichner, K. (2009). Social justice teacher education. In W. Ayers, T. Quinn, & D. Stovall (Eds.), *Handbook of social justice in education* (pp. 595–610). New York, NY: Routledge.

McLaren, P. (2007). *Life in schools: An introduction to critical pedagogy in the foundations of education* (5th ed.). Boston, MA: Pearson Education.

Milner, H. R., IV (2010). *Start where you are, but don't stay there: Understanding diversity, opportunity gaps, and teaching in today's classrooms.* Cambridge, MA: Harvard Education Press.

Moll, L. (1992). Funds of knowledge for teaching: Using a qualitative approach to connect homes and classrooms. *Theory into Practice, 31*(1), 32–41.

Phillion, J., Malewski, E., Rodriguez, E., Shirley, V., Kulago, H., & Bulington, J. (2008). Problems and perils of study abroad: White privilege revival. In T. Huber-Warring (Ed.), *Growing a soul for social change: Building the knowledge base for social justice.* Charlotte, NC: Information Age.

Said, E. W. (2003). *Orientalism.* London, UK: Penguin.

Sartre, J. P. (1984). *Being and nothingness* (H. E. Barnes, Trans.). New York, NY: Washington Square. (Original work published 1943)

Tehranian, J. (2009). *Whitewashed: America's invisible Middle Eastern minority.* New York: New York University Press.

Valenzuela, A. (1999). *Subtractive schooling: U.S.-Mexican youth and the politics of caring.* Albany: State University of New York Press.

Villegas, A. M. & Lucas, T. (2002). Preparing culturally responsive teachers: Rethinking the curriculum. *Journal of Teacher Education, 53*(1), 20–32.

Zeichner, K. M. (2009). *Teacher education and the struggle for social justice.* New York, NY: Routledge.

CHAPTER 5

BEYOND DOMINANT DISCOURSE ON ISLAM

Proposal for Disruptions Through Teacher Education Programs for Democratic Engagement and Social Justice

Amina Shareef and Adrien Chauvet

US and UK citizens should distinguish the faith of mainstream Muslims from the claims of a minority of extremists who justify their acts of violence and terrorism in the name of Islam. Blurring this distinction plays into the hands of preachers of hate (Muslim and non-Muslim) whose rhetoric incites and demonizes, alienates and marginalizes and leads to the adoption of domestic policies that undermine the civil liberties of Muslims and non-Muslims alike.
　　　　—Professor John Esposito, Georgetown University Founding
　　　　Director, Prince Alwaleed bin Talal Center for Muslim-Christian
　　　　Understanding, Professor of religion, international affairs and
　　　　Islamic studies Georgetown University

Teacher Education for Social Justice: Perspectives and Lessons Learned, pages 53–65.
Copyright © 2013 by Information Age Publishing

Let's not ask CNN, ABC, FOX . . . let's not ask the London Times, or the Australian Times . . . let's not ask non-Muslims about how Muslim women feel.
—Khalid Yasin (2007)}

The events of September 11, 2001, effectively hailed in a new era of unwanted visibility for the vast majority of Muslims living in the Western world, because Muslims were accused of engineering the attacks. Although some Muslims practice an extreme form of Islam fundamentally in ideological dissonance with mainstream Islamic practices and beliefs to which the majority of the world's 1.6 billion Muslims adhere, the subsequent media coverage did not highlight this difference, as illustrated by the following:

{EX}Immediately after September 11, the New York Times launched a new section entitled "A Nation Challenged." It continued to appear every day for the next four months. The editors billed it as "searching for the causes" and "committed to complete worldwide coverage of the roots and consequences of September 11." This section, as well as the regular ones and the op-ed pages, ran reams of articles with such potent titles as "Yes, this is about Islam," "This is a religious war," "Jihad 101," "The one true faith," "Dictates of faith," "Defusing the holy bomb," "Barbarians at the gates," "The force of Islam," "Divine inspiration," "The core of Muslim rage," "Dreams of holy war," "Mosque and state," "Word for word: Islam's argument," "The deep intellectual roots of Islamic rage," "The age of Muslim wars," "A head-on collision of alien cultures," "Feverish protests against the West," "How Islam and politics mixed," "Survey of the Islamic World," "Faith and the secular state," "A business plan for Islam Inc," "Hair as a battlefield for the soul," "How Islam won, and lost the lead in science," and "Two views: Can the Koran condone terror?" (Abrahamian, 2003)

Muddying this distinction, the media generated a sense of complicity that consequently resulted in a public sentiment that blamed Muslims at-large for these events. In fact, since 9/11, media coverage on Islam and Muslims continues to blur this radicalized, minority practice of Islam from the democratic, peaceable, mainstream Islam (Powell, 2011). These media discourses create an association between Islam and Muslims with violence and radicalism and essentialize the multiple identities of the adherents of Islam to one informed by Arabic culture and aesthetic (Abrahamian, 2003; Aziz, 2010; Bilici, 2008; Bradford, 2009; L. Jackson, 2010; Moore, 2009; Powell, 2011; Wang, 2009).

To put into perspective the hegemony of this discourse, a study conducted by Cardiff University revealed that two thirds of the media coverage that hit the airwaves in England between 2000 and 2008 described Islam as backward and dangerous, a threat and source of a problem, and the coverage labeled Muslims as extremists, fundamentalists, militants, radicals, and fanatics (Moore, Mason, & Lewis, 2008). Even cursory media analysis reveals that this discourse continues to prevail today. Discourse analysis of the media coverage of the revolutions in the Muslim world that started in Tunisia and purportedly created a domino effect that provoked similar demonstrations in Egypt, Libya, Morocco, Jordan, Syria, Iran, and Yemen highlights just how the media creates the image of Muslims as unstable, reactionary, anti-institution, violent, and incompetent. The use of the words "rebels," "uprising," and "chaos," among other highly connotative diction, to describe the people and their attempt to recuperate democracy from colonial influences, reinstate basic civil liberties, redress social inequities, and resist unjust economic structures demonstrates a calculated framing of events to evoke and perpetuate the association of Muslims with violence.

Additionally, the media rhetoric on the French legislation enacted on April 11, 2011, that would criminalize the wearing of the burqa, a face covering, in public spaces, which would only apply to an insignificant fraction of the French Muslim population (Gabizon, 2009; Galaud, 2009), points at the media's intent to summon and perpetuate the archaic stereotype that Islamic principles oppress Muslim women. Although the burqa, as understood by the overwhelming majority of Islamic scholars, marks a cultural (not Islamic) practice (Ramadan, 2009), which the media insists on defining as the "Islamic veil" (Rustici, 2011), indicates a rhetorical attempt to tie this practice to Islam in order to fan into fury yet another formulaic critique against Islam. In truth, the media articulates an entirely negative discourse on Islam, bantering with the most offensive language that, had similar language been deployed to speak about Blacks, Jews, homosexuals, or women, it would have elicited public outrage; yet this language continues to describe Muslims with very little resistance or outcry (Sardar, 2006). Perhaps the absence of contestation suggests that such ideas have been common-sensical; in other words, this representation has become hegemonic (Powell, 2011).

The questions that remain are as follows: How do these discourses mediate public perception toward Islam, advance a political agenda, and inform the ways in which Muslims identify themselves? What marks the urgency of providing counterdiscourses? How can teacher education programs intervene in disrupting the hegemony of these discourses and what may the counterdiscourses resemble? It is in offering conceptualizations to these questions that we devote the rest of this chapter.

CONSEQUENCES OF MASS MEDIA ISLAM

In describing the consequences of Mass Media Islam, a term coined to describe the version of Islam projected through mainstream media, we will focus on how it particularly shapes three social spheres: the *public sphere*, the *legal sphere*, and the *private sphere*. The public sphere involves the perception of Islam and Muslims by the American people and the subsequent translation of this perception; the legal sphere involves governmental exploitation of these discourses; and the private sphere involves Muslim self-perception and identification.

Studies and research findings reveal that media discourses do indeed shape viewer perceptions of Islam and Muslims—and for large numbers of Americans in negative ways. According to statistics generated by Pew Research Center, 52% of Americans polled (2009b) express concern about a possible rise in Islamic extremism and 35% (August, 2010) continue to believe that Islam is more likely than other religions to encourage violence. This is despite the fact that an overwhelming 78% of American Muslims (2009a) condemn violent acts such as suicide bombings, deeming them as unjustifiable. Additionally, 43% (CAIR, 2011) believe that Islamic beliefs do not encourage respect for followers of different faiths. These numbers signal the internalization of Mass Media Islam of a sizable American population and consequently mark the salience of media in providing the shape of public perspective (Brinson, 2010).

These popularized notions of Islam create a culture of fear, an othering of Muslims that dichotomizes the United States and Islam, and frames Muslims as threats to the American identity as well as homeland security. Subsequently, this results in domestic discrimination and hate crimes against visible Muslims (Powell, 2011). The statistics generated by the Council for American Islamic Relations (CAIR, 2011), a U.S.-based organization that defends Muslim civil liberties, demonstrates the media's toll on American subjectivities. CAIR processed 1,972 complaints of hate crimes against Muslims in 2005. In short, media representation of Islam affects public perception, which in turn affects visible Muslim Americans through discrimination and hate crimes. In light of this, there remains a pressing question: How do anti-Muslim sentiments nurtured by the media play into factors that affect the legal sphere?

By regulating and shaping discourses so that a particular ideology becomes the frame of reference for thought and subsequent discourse, media outlets serve as state apparatuses for mobilizing public support for various governmental proceedings such as the passing of certain legislation and engaging in war (McLaren, 2007).Accordingly, the media representation of Islam is exploited by governmental bodies in order to legislate Draconian laws that infringe on civil liberties such as the Patriot Act in the United States and the hijab, the head covering ban in French public schools in 2005. The media largely holds the responsibility for creating the public sentiment necessary for the passing of legislation that violates democratic principles without widespread resistance.

Not surprisingly, according to a Cornell University study, 44% of Americans polled would support government curtailment of Muslim civil liberties (CAIR, 2011). The French hijab ban serves as a powerful example of media implications on policy in the educational sector as this legislation affectively further marginalized the minority Muslim population in France by limiting access to education to those children who do not practice dominant French culture. Furthermore, it established assimilation as an acceptable pedagogical model in French public schools. By appropriating the oft-cited discourse that the hijab oppresses Muslim women, the media coverage ensured widespread French support for this ban, although such a ban clearly violated core French principles of *liberté d'expression*—freedom of expression. In addition to garnering public support, these discourses frame how police officers, travel security agents, and counterterrorism personnel are trained to respond to Muslims and Muslim communities (Political Research Associate, 2011). Oftentimes, this translates into legitimizing racist means of law enforcement, such as religious profiling at airports, at large Muslim gatherings, and at Islamic schools (CAIR & University of California, Berkeley Center for Race and Gender, 2010). In short, dominant discourses on Islam distributed by the media play an ideological role in securing a popular consent that the state exploits in order to produce unconstitutional laws and to marginalize and target the Muslim community (CAIR & University of CAlifornia, Berkeley Center for Race and Gender, 2010). However, an equally damaging consequence of the media representation of Islam and Muslims is its role in brutalizing the Muslim identity and its implications on Muslim consciousness.

Media representations mediate the process of socialization and identity formation by providing the viewers with the images of socially acceptable roles and behavior that conform to White, middle-class models of normativity, while stigmatizing those that do not. Subsequently, media representation of Islam, in stigmatizing and essentializing the Muslim identity, disrupts the possibility for Muslims to develop positive self-identities (E. J. Jackson, 2009). This disruption inflicts a sort of wound on the collective Muslim psyche (Brinson, 2010) and initiates a psychological crisis expressing a variety of symptoms. Muslims experience liminality—being stranded on the borderlands that are created at the junction of two worlds—desiring, although not receiving, inclusion in either world. They feel self-alienation when their identities become mere performances of socially acceptable identities at the expense of more authentic expressions. And worse, Muslims who feel self-hatred oftentimes reject their historical and cultural origins. In short, these discourses dehumanize the followers of Islam both by labeling Muslims as fundamentally incongruent with universal humanity and causing internalization to this sense of inferiority. These discourses wield the potential to symbolically colonize Muslim consciousness through the consequent fragmentation and weakening (Laing, 2010) of the Muslim identity. This lived psychology in turn affects Muslim willingness to participate in both social and civic spheres and, especially for Muslim children, affects self and academic confidence necessary for educational success in the schooling system. In essence, the media representation of Muslims demands a cultural/religious castration from any practice informed by Islam and sends the underlying message that invisibility is the acceptable way of expressing a Muslim identity in the West.

THE URGENCY OF PROVIDING A COUNTERDISCOURSE TO MASS MEDIA ISLAM

The urgency in providing a counterdiscourse to Mass Media Islam rests not only on Muslim Americans but on non-Muslims alike, as such discourses effectively jeopardize the democratic system at-large in that they resort to fabrication, vilification, and repression of the community *du jour* in determining the shape and structure of society. The abovementioned statistics that describe the percentage of Americans who harbor negative perceptions of Islam and Muslims clearly marks the necessity of challenging discourses that threaten the principles of democratic pluralism. It stands as the objective of multiculturalism to create social spaces wherein the inhabitants understand that the multiplicity of social identities expresses the nature of the human condition so as to arrive at a point of mutual respect and reciprocity, without fear of difference, without ethnocentrism (Banks, 2005). The viability of any democracy is predicated on this conceptualization and engagement with plurality, for the "demo" in democracy does not exclude or privilege a particular population of humanity—it is all-inclusive. Therefore, dominant discourses on Islam pose a threat to democracy because they construct difference as a marker of inferiority, of something fearful, which subsequently undermines the social unity necessary for a collective democracy. As such, these discourses appropriate democracy as a vehicle for social fragmentation instead of a tool for the people's empowerment.

In addition, the discursive manipulation that precedes the mobilization of support for antidemocratic laws and engagement violates every possible conception of democratic citizenship and so endangers the entire edifice of democracy itself. Truly democratic proceedings would unfold through the examination of multiple discourses so that the multiplicity of opinion would inform the collective judgment and consequent legislation. However, with the current media hegemony, as concerns Mass Media Islam or any other discourse, such examination remains far from a possibility and so represents the disintegration of the democratic process. Therefore, the formulation of counterdiscourses serves both to represent the plurality of voices as well as to preserve the conditions within which democracy can even exist. Accordingly, it remains the responsibility of the American people, regardless of religious affiliation, to challenge the hegemony of Mass Media Islam.

On the same note, true democratic pluralism embraces a variegated population in a fashion analogous to the tight weave of a multicolored fabric; cultural differences need not compromise the integrity of the society in the same way the color of a thread does not contribute weakness—only beauty—to the fabric. Accordingly, the psychological trauma inflicted on the Muslim community through the repeated exposure to degrading media representations of Islam and the Muslim identity provokes a reflexive contraction of American Muslims from public spaces into closed communities, in reactive solidarity, which in turn effaces the Muslim identity from the collective, social fabric. This invisibility, both a reaction to and a demand made by dominant discourses, in turn poses a challenge for Muslims, primarily Muslim women, who wish to participate in the larger social spheres, since the hijab makes them very visible; some Muslim women enter the social sphere to become targets of verbal or physical abuse, some women choose to stay in the comfort of their homes, and some women forsake the hijab for social invisibility. In any of the three situations, Muslim women experience multiple oppression. A democratic society would not subject anyone to such oppression on the basis of their identity, as such an occurrence marks the devalorization of multiculturalism—the condition that provides the nutriment from which democracies grow and flourish. In short, the necessity of contesting dominant discourses on Islam remains in its threat to the processes of democratic engagement as well as the circumstances from which democracies prosper. This threat signals the need to interrogate and confront these discourses in multiple sites such as schools and university teacher education programs.

INTERRUPTING DOMINANT DISCOURSES ON ISLAM IN TEACHER EDUCATION PROGRAMS: THE IMAGE OF THESE DISRUPTIONS

As teacher education programs for social justice ideally offer coursework that contextualizes schooling and education within the broader objectives of the various orders that structure society (McDonald & Zeichner, 2009), they therefore provide the space for deconstructing dominant discourses. Programs with a social justice orientation must inform prospective teachers that educational structures are products of specific historical, political, and social contingencies, in order that they may learn the necessity of interrogating and problematizing commonsensical rhetoric surrounding schooling (Cochran-Smith, 2004). As such, teacher education programs for social justice must understand contemporary urgencies and adapt their curricula accordingly. Because Mass Media Islam and its consequences mark one social urgency, it is imperative that teacher education programs employ curricular interventions to critically engage this issue. The dismal absence of such an engagement in current teacher education programs essentially maintains such media discourses—as Applebaum (2009) says, the absence of discourse is discourse itself. And failure to criticize is an indication of approval. The next few paragraphs will describe how teacher education programs may engage dominant discourses on Islam and follow with a description of curricular interventions that teachers can deploy for creating mutual respect among followers of different faiths and spiritualities for constructing identity validating spaces in the classroom.

Islam in Teacher Education Programs

For the most part, multicultural literature, in focusing on how race, class, and gender inform identities, neglects to mention the role religion plays in providing the contours of identity and self-expression. Teacher education literature too, in failing to highlight the salience of religion in people's lives and its consequent shaping of subjectivities, ill-prepare teachers to negotiate diversity in religious expression as well as to create mutual respect for the beliefs and practices of the various faiths and spiritualities observed in the United States (Moore, 2009). It stands as imperative to understand that teachers are hardly exempt from the implicating statistics cited above of the number of Americans who fear Muslims and/or possess negative opinions of Islam. Accordingly, teacher education programs must engage teachers in a process of self-introspection in order to unpack their perceptions of various religious groups living in the United States, as well as to raise awareness of how various institutions, media, schools, religion, and family socialize and frame these perceptions (Cochran-Smith, 2004; Zeichner, 2009). Not only does this process prepare future educators to implement socially just practices in order to accommodate a diversity of religious expressions, but it positions teachers as reflective practitioners who understand how schooling practices and knowledge, in valorizing those of particular groups over others, symbolically dismiss the plurality of being and knowing.

Given the political focus and saturation of the media on Islam and Muslims, preservice teachers must engage a process of personal interrogation that explores their perception of Islam and Muslims. Teacher education programs must provide instructional literature on Islam that recognizes Muslim contributions to Western civilization, details the central tenets of Islam, narrates the history of Islam, describes Muslim American experiences in the United States, and a plethora of other topics to help teachers deconstruct their opinions that have been primarily informed by popular media and to replace the image of the vocal, violent minority with the image of the positive Muslim majority (Moore, 2009). This positive image will preclude differential treatment, low expectations, and negative opinions of Muslim students, which will permit teachers to create socially just classroom conditions that allow all students to potentialize on their native capacities.

Furthermore, teachers will understand when and how to intervene when curriculum or textbooks present a unilateral and demonizing view of Islam and Muslims, to disrupt the propagation of Mass Media Islam. Additionally, such an image will interrupt the false dichotomy of "Islam versus the

West" and convey the idea that both share intertwined, positive histories and that expressing a Muslim identity in the West does not need to demand a distancing or rejection of all things "Western." However, an engagement with religion in teacher education programs does not need to restrict itself to providing literature only on Islam, but it must provide literature for all major faiths and spiritualities in order to promote tolerance and mutual cohabitation, an urgency marked by the fact that 83% of Americans polled claimed to practice some form of religion (Garrett, 2010).

Teaching Mutual Respect Between Followers of Different Religions and Spiritualities in Public Schools

What we advocate moves beyond a focus on dispelling dominant perceptions on Islam and endorses a totalizing project that prepares preservice teachers to negotiate, appreciate, and positively portray various nonmainstream religions and spiritualities such as Islam, Buddhism, Hinduism, Judaism, agnosticism, and atheism. As immigration brings followers of faiths different from Christianity into a predominantly Christian country, part of the challenge of creating a society founded on the principles of inclusion and accommodation requires the recognition of the validity of different religious and spiritual practices. For such societies as our own, which reflect diversity in faith and spiritual observances, if mutual respect and reciprocity are desired, it remains incumbent that schools and teacher education programs engage a curriculum that aims to achieve just that. Such engagements align themselves with the democratic project of creating social unity and serve to maintain the conditions that allow democracy to thrive.

Schools must deploy curricula that expose students to the histories, contributions to civilization, basic beliefs, and cultures of different faiths and spiritualities in a language that neither colonizes nor suggests inferiority or primitivity relative to any other practice. Failure to do so itself is discourse, as it provides an image of nonmainstream faith practices as alien, distant, incomprehensible, primitive, and anti-Western. As such, every course must include description of a said religious group's contribution to that particular subject at hand; for example, biology or chemistry courses would credit the contributors of particular scientific theory or discovery by highlighting their religious affiliation, as would math, geography, astronomy, history, and English courses. Through acknowledging contributors to knowledge by his or her religious identity, students understand the religious diversity behind the laying of the foundations of modern science and contemporary knowledges; this subsequently opens up the possibility for appreciating different religions and narrows the contemporary chasm between peoples of different faiths—a chasm that exists when ignorance of different religions' histories, practices, beliefs, and contributions to life prevail. Additionally, it provides students with positive, self-affirming images that serve to impart a sense of validity to a particular religious identity. Furthermore, it disrupts the hegemony of media discourses that convey distorted information and accordingly promotes the social unity necessary for true democratic engagement. In conclusion, the diversity of religious practices and spiritualities demands that schools intervene in creating mutual respect among followers of different faiths in order to preserve democratic processes in this country.

CONCLUSION

Dominant media streams propagate an image of Islam that does not represent the Islam practiced by the overwhelming majority of the world's 1.6 billion Muslims. This image portrays Islam as violence-inspiring, oppressive to women, and antimodernity and anti-Western, and it depicts Muslims as fundamental fanatics inclined toward terrorism and the destruction of America. As a consequence of repeated exposure to such discourses on Islam, a startling percentage of American people have internalized this negative image to the detriment of Muslim Americans and to the benefit of legislative bodies. Muslim Americans increasingly face discrimination in the workforce, at airports, and in the public sphere. By describing Muslims as a threat needing containment, Mass Media Islam gives legislative bodies the rationale for enacting laws that are unconstitutional and infringe on the basic civil liberties of Muslims. As a result, not only do Muslims experience difficulty in participating in the larger collective, they suffer from the psychological pain inflicted on them through the brutalization of the Muslim identity—pain that produces long-lasting effects on the collective Muslim psyche.

These media discourses signal a deterioration of the democratic process for two reasons: they deploy discursive manipulation in determining the shape and structure of society, and they mark difference as inferior and fearful and so disrupt the expression of multiple perspectives as well as fragment the social cohesion needed for democratic exchange. Consequently, it remains the responsibility of all Americans to provide counterdiscourses to Mass Media Islam as a means of protecting democracy in this country. Teacher education programs that work for social justice must meet the current challenges that various minority groups face. They must impart in preservice teachers the necessity of problematizing schooling media and schooling rhetoric as a means of interrupting the reproduction of marginalizing ideologies and alienating spaces in schools. As such, teacher education programs for social justice must engage Mass Media Islam, as they serve as prime sites for contesting destructive discourses, for restoring the conditions that allow democratic citizenship. Schools and university training programs must respond to the increase in religious diversity in America in order to instill reciprocated trust and tolerance between followers of different faiths and spiritualities.

In short, the conversation on the salience of religion in American lives as well as in providing the skeleton on which identities are dressed must reenter the public and academic discourse in order to meet the urgency of the Muslim American condition and the demands of rising religious diversity. Schools and teacher education programs must reflect this accommodation and strive toward creating the conditions in which peaceful cohabitation among people of various faiths may exist. Unless this occurs, we foresee continued marginalization of people on the basis of a religious identity and the consequent deterioration of the democratic process.

REFERENCES

Abrahamian, E. (2003). The US media, Huntington and September 11. *Third World Quarterly, 24*(3), 529–544.

Applebaum, B. (2009) Is teaching for social justice a liberal bias? *Teachers College Record, 11*(2), 376–408.

Aziz, M. A. (2010). *Maintaining the faith: Factors that promote a Muslim religious identity* (Doctoral dissertation). Retrieved from ProQuest Dissertations and Theses (3419251), http://search.proquest.com/dissertations/docview/755288645/139C668AAE16E715549/1?accountid=13360

Banks, J. A. (2005). Multicultural education: Historical development, dimensions, and practice. In J. A. Banks & C. A, Banks (Eds.), *Handbook of research on multicultural education.* (pp. 3–29). San Francisco, CA: Jossey Bass.

Bilici, M. (2008). *Finding Mecca in America: American Muslims and cultural citizenship* (Doctoral dissertation). Retrieved from ProQuest Dissertations and Theses (3328769), http://search.proquest.com/dissertations/docview/304578540/139C66A6EC715EF93/1?accountid=13360

Bradford, J. W. (2009). *American/Muslim: Reactive solidarity, identity politics and social identity formation in the aftermath of September 11th.* (Doctoral dissertation). Retrieved from ProQuest Doctoral Dissertations and Theses. (3350949), http://search.proquest.com/dissertations/docview/304894061/previewPDF/139C66B840551F8FF46/1?accountid=13360

Brinson, M. E. (2010). *Muslims in the media: Social and identity consequences for Muslims in America* (Doctoral dissertation). Retrieved from ProQuest Doctoral Dissertations and Theses (3427827, http://search.proquest.com/dissertations/docview/815629298/139C66DA3295F982470/1?accountid=13360

Council on American-Islamic Relations (CAIR) & University of California, Berkeley Center for Race and Gender. (2010). *Islamophobia and its Impact in the United States. Same Hate, New Target.* Washington, DC.

Cochran-Smith, M. (2004). *Walking the road: Race, diversity, and social justice in teacher education.* New York, NY: Teacher's College Press.

Council on American-Islamic Relations (CAIR). (2011, May 2). *Islamophobia and anti-Americanism.* Retrieved from http://www.cair.com/Issues/Islamophobia/Islamophobia.aspx

Gabizon, C. (2009, August 9). Deux mille femmes portent la burqa en France. *Le Figaro.* Retrieved from http://www.lefigaro.fr/actualite-france/2009/09/09/01016-20090909ARTFIG00040-deux-mille-femmes-portent-la-burqa-en-france-.php

Galaud, F. (2009, July 30). La burqa, Un phenomena marginal en France. *Le Figaro.* Retrieved from http://www.lefigaro.fr/actualite-france/2009/07/30/01016-20090730ARTFIG00202-la-burqa-un-phenomene-marginal-en-france-.php

Garrett, S. R. (2010). *American grace: How religion divides and unites us.* New York, NY: Simon & Schuster.

Jackson, E. J. (2009). *Teaching about controversial groups in public schools: Critical multiculturalism and the case of Muslim since September 11.* (Doctoral dissertation). Retrieved from ProQuest Dissertation and Theses (3392076), http://search.proquest.com/dissertations/docview/304895566/139C66E6AB749BBAA7F/1?accountid=13360

Jackson, L. (2010). Images of Islam in U.S. media and their educational implications. *Educational Studies, 46,* 3–24.

Laing, C. J. (2010). *The Muslim identity crisis: Sharia as a mechanism for decolonization.* (Thesis). Retrieved from ProQuest Doctoral Dissertations and Theses, http://search.proquest.com/dissertations/docview/759483040/139C66F71E8ED2C3DC/1?accountid=13360

McDonald, M., & Zeichner, K. (2009). Social justice teacher education. In W. Ayers, T. Quinn, & D. Stovall (Eds), *Handbook of social justice in education* (pp. 595–610). New York, NY: Routledge.

McLaren, P. (2005). *Life in schools: An introduction to critical pedagogy in the foundations of education.* New York and London: Longmans.

Moore, J. R. (2009). Why religious education matters: The role of Islam in multicultural education. *Multicultural Perspectives, 11*(3), 139–145.

Moore, K., Mason, P., & Lewis, J. (2008). *The representation of British Muslims in the national print news media 2000–2008.* Cardiff, Wales: Cardiff School of Journalism, Media and Cultural Studies.

Pew Research Center Publications. (2010, August 24). *Public remains conflicted over Islam.* Retrieved from http://pewresearch.org/pubs/1706/poll-americans-views-of-muslims-object-to-new-york-islamic-center-islam-violence

Pew Research Center Publications. (2009a, December 17). *Little support for terrorism among Muslim Americans.* Retrieved from http://pewresearch.org/pubs/1445/little-support-for-terrorism-among-muslim-americans

Pew Research Center Publications. (2009a, November 18). *Modest rise in concern about Islamic extremism.* Retrieved from http://pewresearch.org/pubs/1414/concerns-about-islamic-extremism

Political Research Associate. (2011). *Manufacturing the Muslim menace: Private firms, public servants, and the threat to rights and security.* Retrieved from www.public-eye.org/liberty/training/Muslim_Menace_Complete.pdf

Powell, K. A. (2011). Framing Islam: An analysis of U.S. media coverage of terrorism since 9/11. *Communication Studies, 62*(1), 90–112.

Ramadan, T. (2009, October 23). *Is the burqa compatible with a Western society?* Retrieved from http://www.tariqramadan.com

Rustici, C. (2011, April 12). *French ban on veils prompts defiance.* Retrieved from http://articles.boston.com/2011-04-12/news/29410685_1_veils-muslim-women-french-ban

Sardar, Z. (2006). If journalists described Jews or gay people as they do Muslims, they would be hounded out of what is left of Fleet Street. *Journalism Studies, 7*(1), 34–47.

Wang, Y. (2009). *An uncertain future: Negotiating multiple identities in a racially and ethnically diverse mosque in the post 9.11 United States.* (Doctoral dissertation). Retrieved from ProQuest Doctoral Dissertations and Theses (3441766), http://search.proquest.com/dissertations/docview/851714781/139C670A1C23C40 6ADA/1?accountid=13360

Yasin, K. (2007, July 26). Let's not ask non-Muslims about Muslim women. *YouTube.* Retrieved from http://www.youtube.com/watch?v=cxFKSC0c_UY

Zeichner, K. M. (2009). *Teacher education and the struggle for social justice.* New York, NY: Routledge.

CHAPTER 6

IDENTITY AND SOCIAL JUSTICE DEVELOPMENT OF PRESERVICE TEACHERS

Maricela Alvarado and Amy Carey

The research in social justice education for preservice teachers is growing and continues to question the responsibilities of collegiate education programs and development of curriculum to reflect social justice pedagogy. According to Cochran-Smith (2010), "Some programs emphasize teachers' beliefs and identity, others focus on democratic education, and many others concentrate on multicultural issues" to incorporate social justice pedagogy into their programs (p. 445). This chapter provides a working theory of social justice identity development for preservice teachers. We believe that this theory will provide sequential levels of social justice pedagogy inserted into the curriculum or program resulting in continual development for preservice teachers. Using various methods and theories of identity development, we draw from the work Chickering's Seven Vectors (Chickering & Reisser, 1993). We also focus primarily on college student development with which critical analysis began in the late 1960s and early 1970s as a result of the Civil Rights Movement and many college student uprisings during the Vietnam War (p. 44). College student development deserves

Teacher Education for Social Justice: Perspectives and Lessons Learned, pages 67–79.
Copyright © 2013 by Information Age Publishing

scholarly attention from teacher education programs and practical use, as does the teaching practices and child development in our K–12 system.

There are three general stages we describe in this chapter: internal, external, and reflection. We use the term *stages* not to imply a static position or a linear model but suggest this theory be used as a continual movement to, from, and through self-reflection and sociopolitical consciousness/action in education (Helms, 1995). The social justice paradigm implies that justice evolves from within, organically, and reflects the needs of the community from which it evolves (Jaramillo, 2010). Not all preservice teachers return to the communities they have known and grown up with; therefore, they must be able to move and become a part of the community they will be teaching in. Ultimately, the goal of this theory is to provide a framework through which preservice educators understand the processes they must move continually through in order to evolve with social justice education as a baseline for their own teacher preparation development. Cochran-Smith (2004) also asserts that inquiry should happen at all stages of development (p. 52).

We begin working from the internal, preservice teachers reflecting on one's own educational experiences and consciousness of race and class issues. Moving to the external, we suggest that preservice teachers can then work from a personal cultural framework to analyze, interpret, and critique education systems and the politics that surround them. Lastly, we theorize that the preservice teacher would then have opportunities to put social justice theory to practice. Preservice teachers could then use community inquiry to further inform their knowledge and experiences. To incorporate this identity-development theory, it would need programwide support from faculty and administrators. With that support, we propose that assessment could work alongside this theory as a way to gauge a program's effectiveness and preservice teacher development.

IDENTITY-DEVELOPMENT FRAMEWORKS

Many social justice frameworks provide different ideas for teachers to use in working with their preservice teachers, although they do not directly address preservice teachers' identity development in teacher education programs. For example, Cochran-Smith (2004) uses her five perspectives on race, culture, and language diversity, including "reconsidering personal knowledge and experience, locating teaching with the culture of school and the community, analyzing children's learning opportunities, understanding children's understanding, and constructing reconstructionist pedagogy" as essential knowledge for teachers (p. 49). While there is an abundance of work that provides theory and pedagogy as to why we should have social justice as a basis of education programs and how to use social justice in the broader sense of teaching, there is value in providing a theory to identity development specifically addressing the collegiate experience of preservice teachers. While analyzing the K–12 social justice frameworks, we found relevance in regard to preservice teachers' inquiry and developing knowledge of educational systems they are encountering, have encountered, or will encounter.

Self-Awareness Before External Awareness

In our search for an identity-development model for preservice teachers, we found evidence of the importance of teachers' developing self-awareness before they develop external or structural awareness. One work specifically demonstrated how preparation through self-reflection before fieldwork may positively influence practical experience.

Phillion et al. (2008) wrote of a group of preservice teachers who were participating in a study abroad wherein they experienced rural Honduran schools. The promise, as Phillion et al. described it, is in providing teachers with cultural and language immersion in preparation for working with underserved populations in the United States. The goal then is to help preservice teachers develop external and structural awareness; they are provided with an experience with the potential to help them develop empathy and knowledge of the biases and social injustices that may take place externally. In the postprogram interviews, the perils of the program were revealed. Two separate participants actually reinforced their own privileged position by externalizing poverty and feeling "blessed" by their own circumstances, in contrast to recognizing that poverty exists throughout their own country and recognizing the White privilege they have benefitted from. Phillion et al. aptly summarized, "In each of these cases, the participants were unable, and possibly unwilling to recognize their Whiteness, and therefore unable to associate it with privilege" (p. 379). The implication we draw from these findings is the need for self-reflection and awareness of personal privileges and biases to begin before preservice teachers begin to develop external or structural awareness. Simply sending preservice teachers abroad and hoping they develop empathy and the ability to critically analyze privilege is not enough. The curriculum must work in tandem with the goals of a study-abroad or experiential learning activity so that the preservice teachers' experiences are maximized.

Building External Awareness Through Fieldwork

Similar to internal awareness, practical experience and ongoing professional development are key in developing culturally responsive teachers. Shoffner and Brown (2010) wrote of the experience of a first-year teacher's struggle to be culturally responsive to his student body. They describe how a preservice teacher who was well prepared still struggled to enact culturally responsive pedagogy. They noted, "Culturally responsive teaching, specifically, requires a breadth of knowledge and a depth of understanding of students, pedagogy, self and community that few teachers can assimilate in the early years of their career" (p. 108). This supports the idea that gaining practical experience and having access to mentors both as preservice teachers and beyond is important, even if preservice teachers are well prepared. Lucas, Villegas, and Freedson-Gonzalez (2008) offered another example of the ability to build external awareness through preservice experience. The authors suggested that in order for teachers to be linguistically responsive, they must experience working with English language learners (ELLs): "Without such contact, ELLs will remain an abstraction . . . Direct contact allows future teachers to see ELLs as individuals, and gives teachers to be a sense of the diversity among ELLs" (p. 370). Both articles provide specific examples of how preservice experience allows future teachers opportunity to learn and build their external and structural awareness with the support of mentors and teachers.

Learning From Collegiate Identity-Development Models

College identity-development models exist in many forms. When looking at higher education scholarly work, we can use Chickering's (Chickering & Reisser, 1993) seven vectors, Helm's (1995) White Racial Identity development model, and many others that examine Black, Latino, LGBTQ, and feminist identity development at the collegiate level. Most of these models and theories begin with (self) awareness and typically end with an identity grounded in inquiry, questioning the status quo with confidence and maturity. Working from Helm's analysis of White racial identity development, it's important to understand what we describe as stages are not levels that preservice teachers reach or accomplish and move on, but they are stages that preservice teachers move to, from, and through continuously. Preservice teachers should achieve the understanding that they should continuously self-reflect, critique, and analyze their environments, especially those that involve their teaching profession.

Chickering's (Chickering & Reisser, 1993) seven vectors are a great basis for college identity development and are widely used by higher education scholars. Chickering aptly described the university's responsibility to incorporate preservice teacher development theory at all levels:

> Student development theory must apply to this generation of students as well as to future ones. It must be useful to institutional leaders as they cope with retrenchment as well as expansion. Without a developmental philosophy at the core of the college, it can become a dispensary of services, a training ground for jobs that don't exist, or a holding tank for those not sure what to do next. Institutions that impart transferable skills and relevant knowledge, bolster

confidence and creativity, and engender social responsibility and self-directed learning are needed more than ever. To be effective in educating the whole student, colleges must hire and reinforce staff members who understand what student development looks like and how to foster it. (p. 44)

The seven vectors are

1. *Developing competence,* which includes intellectual, physical, and interpersonal competence. Intellectual competence derives from academic ability and critical thinking. Physical competence involves personal self-awareness of health, athletic ability, and ability to use creative and artistic self-expression. Interpersonal competence is the ability to socialize, develop leadership skills, and to work effectively in teams.

2. *Managing emotions* involves the ability to understand one's own feelings and emotions, while accepting them and working toward managing emotions effectively for personal and professional success.

3. *Moving through autonomy toward interdependence* is simply one's progress toward self-confidence to direct one's own lives yet understanding the need to be connected to community. The preservice teacher at this stage may form political and social views to reflect their development.

4. *Developing mature interpersonal relationships* is a development of appreciation for human diversity and the ability to establish meaningful long-term relationships.

5. *Establishing identity* is the process that the preservice teacher has already been undertaking in the previous vectors. However, preservice teachers may begin or further attach to certain aspects of their identity that shapes their interests and interpersonal relationships, such as gender, sexual orientation, or cultural heritage.

6. *Developing purpose* is a stage which one moves to developing purpose professionally and personally by making clear and lasting commitments to reflect their identity development.

7. *Developing integrity* includes three stages identified by Chickering as "humanizing values, personalizing values, and developing congruence." The humanizing of values is recognizing a vast value system and relating to those values personally. Personalizing values is identifying values that affirm one's identity yet still acknowledges and respects the values of others. Developing congruence is when one's values are combined with social awareness then moves to action, which forms a solid sense of civic responsibility (Chickering & Reisser, 1993).

These vectors broadly define what a college experience should incorporate. Chickering provides this framework for administrators to better understand the college experience so that the university can provide deliberate actions to enhance this experience and deliver results that benefit both the preservice teacher and the university.

We propose that these vectors should also be considered to incorporate into education programs by both faculty and staff. Preservice teachers who develop competence begin to understand the challenges of higher education that might include a change in attitude toward their study skills and habits developed around those skills leading to academic success. Competence is further achieved when one realizes that academic success is also achieved by staying healthy and incorporating regular practices of stress relief such as working out. The balance of this vector is fully achieved when a preservice teacher can also balance a social life, which may include leadership in student organizations or joining a fraternity or sorority. During the collegiate experience, preservice teachers may be developing their own awareness and management of their emotions by experiencing new relationships such as having a roommate or working in teams. Managing emotions moves into autonomy toward interdependence, which will contribute to the preservice teacher's ability to solve problems with confidence yet recognizing the importance of maintaining or developing relationships. Developing mature interpersonal relationships is important for the preservice teacher in developing cultural and diversity-of-values appreciation. For example, a preservice teacher who has never travelled outside of Indiana, not even to Chicago, should not only experience diversity but should be taught in their course of study how to appreciate differences and relate them to their core values and experiences. Preservice teachers should also be establishing their identity as they develop and grow throughout their college career and beyond. Preservice teachers should learn how to develop purpose that relates to their growing identity. For example, preservice teachers who chooses business because they want to make money may reexamine their life purpose and values as they might relate to their career. Developing this life purpose leads to one's integrity and confidence in self to move toward action, relating to their values and civic responsibility. Such as with teaching, it is important for preservice teacher teachers to understand the environments they will be teaching in and how their life purpose, identity, and value systems relate, thus attaining the confidence to address the possible injustices they encounter. While these vectors aren't meant to be linear, they are interconnected, and we should expect that preservice teachers would move forward, back, and through them. Chickering (Chickering & Reisser, 1993) suggests that college faculty and staff should understand and incorporate these vectors into curriculum planning environmental aspects of the college experience.

RESOLVING TENSIONS THROUGH SEQUENCED IDENTITY-DEVELOPMENT THEORY

There is often tension in preservice education programs regarding the concrete and abstract knowledge needed to teach. Pollock, Deckman, Mira, and Shalaby (2010) described this as one of the three "What can I do?" tensions constantly arising in a teacher education for social justice class. There are many arguments for both theoretical and practical knowledge within the field of teacher education for social justice. A second "What can I do?" question arising in Pollock's work reflects preservice teachers' structural barriers within the school system, and the third is personal barriers. This chapter builds on the arguments above to work toward a sequenced preservice development theory that utilizes both theoretical and practical experiences in progression to help teachers build the tools to answer the "What can I do?" questions that arise.

STAGES FOR PRESERVICE TEACHER IDENTITY DEVELOPMENT

Internal Awareness

The first stage begins with self-reflection—analyzing one's own experiences, biases, and cultural framework (Chubbuck, 2010). A cultural framework can be described as one's background and upbringing. For example, Chubbuck (2010) described the frequently experienced emotions of members of a dominant culture: "guilt, depression, anxiety, and powerlessness" and the frequently experienced emotions of "frustration, and discouragement" by "teachers of color" as they begin the process of self-reflection (p. 203). The importance of recognizing a broader cultural framework as opposed to more obvious attributes such as race and socioeconomic status is also to recognize the infinite number of unique frameworks from which others exist.

During this stage, preservice teachers begin by analyzing their own privileges and internalized biases. We argue that this process is the first stage of identity awareness as it relates to teacher education for social justice. This is supported by Chubbuck's (2010) argument that the process of becoming aware of one's experience and possible privilege is the first step in becoming a teacher for social justice. We theorize this as the first stage of the identity-development process because the preservice teachers' ability to recognize one's privilege and biases allows for a broadened view and sets the stage for broader external inquiry. In talking about denial of male privilege, McIntosh (1990) stated, "These denials protect male privilege from being fully acknowledged, lessened or ended" (p. 31). In the formation of an identity, one cannot be fully equipped to lessen or end the injustices of the classroom and beyond without first being able to acknowledge those injustices from which they may have benefitted. As mentioned above, this process can be difficult and evoke strong emotions. Chubbuck (2010) suggested that teachers acknowledge the emotional strain of this task and helping preservice teachers through it by normalizing the process and modeling the stance of ongoing internal reflection.

The stage of internal or self-awareness is especially important in the education climate today wherein the current teacher population is homogenous and not reflective of student demographics (Zeichner, 2009, p. 408). Teachers whose cultural framework is dissimilar from those of their students may live in a different world, unable to function as a role model, and teach from a deficit perspective (Cochran-Smith, 2004, p. 6). Without acknowledgement of their own cultural framework, White, middle-class teachers may never be able to appropriately respond to the needs of their student body. Cochran-Smith (2004) also argues the importance of self-reflection in "Understanding the racial narrative that underlies a curriculum" (p. 98), which provides the example of a teacher education curriculum recognizing "we" as White women of color learning to educate the "other." Without true critical self-reflection of our own identity, recognizing a curriculum that creates a "we and they" tension may not be possible.

External Educational Systems and Politics

This stage presents the examination of systematic biases in education and political systems. Preservice teachers may be encouraged to conduct some fieldwork through experiences of being placed in situations unfamiliar to their backgrounds and cultures, such as attending community events that highlight culture through education or simply through practicum teaching. Social justice pedagogy (Cochran-Smith, 2004) asserts that teachers must "regard teaching as a political activity and embrace social change as part of the job, teachers who enter the profession not expecting to carry on business as usual but prepared to join other educators and parents in major reforms" (p. 46). This stage reflects this notion of teaching as political. Multicultural classes or tracks provide opportunities for such culture through education experiences. Study abroad is strongly encouraged at this stage because of the aspect of full immersion into a culture as a minority. Study abroad is also a great way to better understand the challenges of English language learners (Phillion et al., 2008). However, teacher education curricula often only provide these opportunities as optional, and when made mandatory, teacher educators may experience resistance. If a curriculum has social justice and a preservice teacher identity-development process ingrained collaboratively and complementarily, this may be alleviated because it will be an expectation of both preservice teachers and professors that they must partake in this type of curriculum. According to Cochran-Smith (2004), localizing experiences can also add to a preservice teacher experience and provide simpler access for inquiry (p. 3). Looking at several education programs across the country, we can use the University of Illinois-Chicago's education program (University of Chicago, 2011) as an example of a social justice-embedded curriculum. Both the preservice teacher and teacher educator would enter the program understanding those expectations of learning and understanding aspects of privilege, systemic biases, and such. During this stage, preservice teachers may find themselves angry and confused by educational systems that contradict the notion of students (or children) first. The intention in this stage would be to have preservice teachers at a level of openness and acceptance, not simply tolerance. The word *tolerance* has been used in higher education diversity programming to encourage understanding of an otherness from self; however, tolerance could also simply be defined as tolerating someone's difference rather understanding and being open to accepting those differences.

Action, Continual Inquiry

At this stage, the preservice teacher has been able to critically self-reflect and analyzes systematic challenges to social justice and equality in education. According to Cochran-Smith (2004), "Inquiry stance" is another way of working toward action for future teachers to feel confident in their grounding of "changing cultures of school reform and competing agendas" (p. 14). Preservice teachers should recognize and be prepared to act according to how "Power, privilege, and economic advantage and/or disadvantage play major roles in the school and home lives of students whether they are part of language, cultural, or gender majority groups or minority groups in our society" (p. 18). Preservice teachers thus can work to take action and participate as a change agent in their fieldwork or practicum experiences. Cochran-Smith identifies perspectives on race, culture, and language diversity and one perspective, *constructing reconstructionist pedagogy*, adds to this stage, as it explains, "Pedagogy is intended to help children understand and then prepare to take action against the social and institutional inequities that are embedded in our society" (p. 59). Preservice teachers may also be educated in participating in leadership and community inquiry (p. 59) as part of their development and continual inquiry into their profession. This stage may also use "action research" to help with their development and continual inquiry (Zeichner, 2009, p. 1600).

It is recommended that at each stage and throughout the curriculum, a mentor or mentors be identified to provide support throughout their growth. As Sleeter (2009) noted, providing guided fieldwork serves the purpose of learning about communities different from the preservice teacher's own, helping them take continual inquiry as a stance, so as to avoid "reinforce[ing] negative stereotypes" (p. 619). A mentor's purpose is to introduce the inquiry community to the student and learn alongside them. Cochran-Smith (2004) described the role: "Experienced teachers and university supervisors work along with prospective teachers to make their own struggles and their own ongoing learning visible and accessible to others and thus offer their own learning as grist for the learning of others" (p.13). Mentors, then, scaffold the continual inquiry and action rather than evaluate the "correctness" of the student's experience.

The stages for preservice identity development of preservice teachers provides a framework for teacher educators and education program curriculums to use when incorporating social justice theory. Using this framework and Chickering's seven vectors (Chickering & Reisser, 1993), preservice teachers will move through their collegiate experience and through an education program understanding their own experiences through this identity-development process. Social justice action requires one to be passionate, relating to the challenges they may confront in their teaching careers. Passion and relatability begin with self; therefore, this framework provides an understanding of self-reflection and awareness, moving toward examination of the external, which is the environment with which they work, live, and such. And finally, the preservice teacher will use the examination of the self internal and environment external to then move to action. Continual inquiry is what provides and allows this framework not to be linear but circular and fluid to move in and through these stages. The stages incorporated in an education curriculum provide the preservice teacher with tools to use and practice with during their course of study and beyond in their profession.

OUTCOMES AND ASSESSMENT

The intended outcomes of this identity-development theory and practice is to produce teachers with social justice at the core of their teaching practices and to ultimately encourage them to not only understand educational inequities but to act against those inequities. We hope to assist what Gay & Kirkland (2003) have termed a "cultural consciousness," which helps preservice teachers identify and acknowledge that "all persons have multiple identities and have life histories structured by race, class, culture, and other aspects of existing societal systems of privilege and oppression" (Cochran-Smith, 2010). Cochran-Smith uses "interpretive frames" to exemplify that "teaching practice is aimed at justice, teachers interpret their work through an inquiry stance by questioning their own and others' assumption, posing and researching problems, and using curricula, tests, and research as generative rather prescriptive" (p. 456). Preservice teachers would then likely be able to address the issues of individual or groups of students that they teach. Therefore, culturally relevant pedagogy can be effectively applied. The challenges will continue to be legislation, meritocracy, and testing. Should a teacher preparation program fully incorporate both social justice and this identity-development theory into their curriculum, there can be effective assessment that would follow a teacher postgraduation. The outcomes and assessment can then provide valuable knowledge on how to improve respective teacher education programs. Assessment and outcomes can be determined and established from the recruitment phase through graduation and beyond.

It is important to have an effective recruitment process that can identify the preservice teachers' strengths and level of knowledge relative to social justice for education. These preservice teachers may also be provided with a mentor as they enter the teacher education program so that they can be supported through their identity-development process. Mentoring could extend beyond graduation to the first professional teaching experience. In that professional phase, it would be beneficial to collect data on their perceptions of their preparation programs. Finally, in order to be able to have long-term assessment, following preservice teachers throughout their teacher career, reporting their development, leadership, and accomplishments would provide valuable data to improve education curriculums. We recognize the difficulty of this long-term assessment and would need administrative and monetary commitment by the program to achieve these goals.

RECOMMENDATIONS

We recommend that education programs for teacher preparation take into serious consideration the processes of identity development of college students and to look to scholarly work from their colleagues in college student development or higher education. Student affairs and development can greatly inform and apply to a social justice curriculum and program for preservice teachers, as they have the same goals in common: to produce a preservice teacher with a confident explored identity that identifies and analyzes injustices and sociocultural factors that affect society and the world. The stages for preservice identity development provides an intentional effort for preservice teachers to examine their own experiences and those of the systems with which they work and live in. Cochran-Smith (2004) explains, "Students cannot teach effectively against the grain if they do not have a thoughtful understanding of what 'the grain' is and what its strength as well as weaknesses are" (p. 63). Many teacher education programs incorporate social justice into their mission/vision statements; however, respective programs must reflect on themselves to ask if they achieve the goals of their missions/visions. We recommend incorporating social justice pedagogy and this identity-development theory into the fabric of the program, wherein the mission/vision is understood and achieved at all levels of the program. As we demonstrate in the outcomes and assessment section, we strongly recommend mentoring as part of the student development process and to help gauge the effectiveness of the teacher education program goals of social justice.

CONCLUSION

This identity-development model for preservice teachers is designed to assist education program curricula, preservice teacher educators, and preservice teachers themselves. We propose that there are essential components needed to be successful in moving through the identity-development stages that were discussed in this chapter. As students studying preservice education, we found ourselves reexamining our own development of awareness, action, and continual inquiry. We realize there are many aspects of identity not fully addressed in this chapter, such as race, ethnicity, gender, sexual orientation, ability, and such. However, we hope that this theory can provide a basic framework for forming other identity theories relative to preservice teacher education. There is a need to identify and validate the processes of development because they can be traumatic, emotional, and life changing. We attempt to assist in preparing teachers for their dynamic environments so they can respond to them with confidence, reflection, and critical analysis. First becoming aware of our own biases and cultural framework is necessary to being open to relating to, understanding, and analyzing the external systematic and political effects on education at all levels. We focus on preservice teachers in the K–12 arena but also feel that the information is transferrable to different areas, such as administrative and community leadership.

REFERENCES

Chickering, A. W., & Reisser, L. (1993). *Education and identity*. San Francisco, CA: Jossey-Bass.

Chubbuck, S. M. (2010). Individual and structural orientations in socially just teaching: Conceptualization, implementation, and collaborative work. *Journal of Teacher Education, 61*(3), 197–210.

Cochran-Smith, M. (2004). *Walking the road: Race, diversity, and social justice in teacher education*. New York, NY: Teachers College Press.

Cochran-Smith, M. (2010). Toward a theory of teacher education for social justice. In A. Hargreaves et al. (Eds.), *Second international handbook of educational change* (pp. 445–467). New York, NY: Springer.

Gay, G., & Kirkland, K. (2003). Developing cultural critical consciousness and self-reflection in preservice teaching. *Theory Into Practice, 42*, 181–187.

Helms, J. E. (1995). An update on Helms' White and people of color racial identity models. In J. G. Ponterotto, J. M. Casas, L. A. Suzuki, & G. M. Alexander (Eds.), *Handbook of multicultural counseling* (pp. 181–198). Thousand Oaks, CA: Sage.

Jaramillo, N. (2010). Social justice for human development. *Teacher Education and Practice, 23*(4), 492–494.

Lucas, T., Villegas, A. M., & Freedson-Gonzalez, M. (2008). Linguistically responsive teacher education: Preparing classroom teachers to teach English language learners. *Journal of Teacher Education, 59,* 361–373.

McIntosh, P. (1990). White privilege: Unpacking the invisible knapsack. *Independent School, 49,* 31–36.

Phillion, J., Malewski, E., Rodriguez, E., Shirley, V., Kulago, H., & Bulington, J. (2008). Promise and perils of study abroad: White privilege revival. In T. Huber-Warring (Ed.), *Growing a soul for social change: Building the knowledge base for social justice.* Charlotte, NC: Information Age.

Pollock, M., Deckman, S., Mira, M., & Shalaby, C. (2010). ''But what can I do?'': Three necessary tensions in teaching teachers about race. *Journal of Teacher Education, 61*(3), 211–224.

Shoffner, M., & Brown, M. (2010). From understanding to application: The difficulty of culturally responsive teaching as a beginning English teacher. In L. Scherff & K. Spector (Eds.), *Culturally relevant pedagogy: Clashes and confrontations* (pp. 89–112). Lanham, MD: Rowman & Littlefield.

Sleeter, C. (2009). Teacher education, neoliberalism, and social justice. In W. Ayers, T. Quinn, & D. Stovall (Eds), *Handbook of social justice in education* (pp. 611–624). New York, NY: Routledge.

University of Illinois-Chicago's Office of Programs and Academic Assessment. (2011). *Curriculum and Instruction.* Retrieved from: http://www.uic.edu/ucat/courses/CI.html

Zeichner, Z. (2009). *Teacher education and the struggle for social justice* [Kindle ed.]. New York, NY: Routledge.

CHAPTER 7

A SOCIAL JUSTICE
CURRICULUM FOR APPALACHIA

Ryan Angus and Joshua Iddings

The Appalachian region of the United States is in a state of crisis. Economically downtrodden, its citizens, in general, make less money, have poorer health, have less education, and have fewer opportunities for improvement than many others in the United States. Schools in this region tend to be underperformers as well, often falling well below national averages on standardized assessments (National Center for Education Statistics, 2009). Despite such realities, it is not the case that teachers and students in Appalachia do not care about education. Educators in the region not only face the normal challenges of education within their schools, but must also deal with the harsh material realities of their region. Rampant poverty and subsequent lack of resources in the region negatively affect literacy abilities, and this in turn affects the ability of Appalachians to bring about change in their material realities. This connection between education and economics is significant in all regions of the United States but is especially salient in Appalachia. For these reasons, among others, Appalachian teachers must adopt an orientation that enables them to see how "their everyday teach-

Teacher Education for Social Justice: Perspectives and Lessons Learned, pages 81–90.
Copyright © 2013 by Information Age Publishing

ing practice is connected to issues of social continuity, change, equity, and social justice" (Zeichner, 2009, p. 54).

In general, but especially in an Appalachian context, social justice calls for equal access to knowledge, opportunities, and financial and material resources, among others. When we look at social justice in an educational context, we must consider both access and equity. Regardless of factors such as race, SES level, or locality, students deserve equal access to knowledge and equal access to the same educational and employment opportunities as students in more "privileged" contexts. Because much of the existing inequity experienced by students is systematic—coming from various laws, policies, and institutional structures—one of the only entry points into student advocacy resides with teachers who can act directly as agents of change in the lives of their students (Villegas & Lucas, 2002). Because of their intermediary position between students and administrators (who, within the school structure, act as a representative and enforcer of policy), teachers are uniquely situated to advocate for students through social justice practices (Achinstein & Athanases, 2010; Ayers, 2004). With all of the abovementioned challenges in Appalachian educational contexts, it is clear that teachers who wish to practice social justice in their classrooms and local contexts have a difficult task in front of them. How can teachers in the region successfully address so many different problems with limited time and resources? Before offering some answers to this question, it would be useful to look in more detail at the Appalachian region itself and the particular nature of the social and economic oppression that happens there.

We recognize that it is still possible that many U.S. citizens might ask where Appalachia is, and in reality, the definition of Appalachia has been debated for many years. Modern definitions of Appalachia, such as those proposed by the Appalachian Regional Commission (ARC), consider the region to be composed of "13 states, 420 counties, 205,000 sq. miles, and 24.8 million people" (ARC, 2010). Williams (2002) designates a smaller part of the ARC's conception of Appalachia as "the regional core" (pp. 13–14). This core is composed of most of West Virginia, western Virginia, eastern Kentucky, eastern Tennessee, western North Carolina, and a portion of northern Georgia, and features the Allegheny/Cumberland mountain ranges to the north, the Blue Ridge Mountains to the south, and the Great Valley region in the middle (Williams, 2002). Historically, this area has been the most disadvantaged in the Appalachian region. According to a recent report issued by the ARC (2010), despite recent growth in Appalachia overall, economic growth in the core region has remained stifled, especially in West Virginia and the eastern Kentucky Cumberland Plateau region.

Statistics concerning educational attainment in this area are also sobering. In core regions like the Cumberland Plateau in Kentucky, only approximately 50% of the people have finished high school. Only about 25% have *attended* college, as compared with 50% nationally (ARC, 2010). In the face of such alarming data, social justice issues and practices become even more significant. In order to more fully understand social justice in an Appalachian context however, we must understand the social and environmental contexts that form the lived experiences of teachers and students in the region.

There are many material conditions that affect and oppress the teachers and students of Appalachia. However, it could be argued that the most significant factor in their oppression is nothing material. Instead, the greatest force in their oppression is discursive. These people are imprisoned by discourses that tend to support industry and progress (the progress of industry). When we look at Appalachia, we must ask what knowledge is valued here and who has control of this knowledge? Who in this area defines and controls social "norms?" Outsiders to the region may find it strange that with all of the abuses suffered at the hands of extractive industries, most people view them positively. People in Appalachia commonly talk about being "pro-coal," and if one says anything bad about the coal industry, it is interpreted as a kind of sacrilege. The sacrosanct coal industry is a master of controlling its own discourse. Over time, coal companies have convinced the citizens around them that they are not only important but absolutely necessary and that the way they do business is the "only" way. Many people believe that these companies care for them, and they are blind to all of their unethical behaviors. As an example, we have heard people who work for Massey Energy say that the company is great because they do things like hosting a large company picnic with fair rides and a concert. How easily, it seems, people acquiesce in the face of injustice.

Although areas in the regional core are not "third world countries," there are many similarities. Altbach (1971) reminds us that

> Colonial powers seldom set up *adequate educational facilities in their colonies and immediately limited educational opportunity* and, in a sense, *hindered modernization* . . . the inadequacies of the modern educational system, *outmoded trends in curriculum*, and the orientation of the schools toward building up an administrative cadre *rather than technically trained and socially aware individuals needed for social and economic development* can be linked in many countries to the colonial experience. [emphasis added]

Viewing Appalachia in this way—as an oppressed area colonized by those in power—can be an insightful way to make sense of the many discourses circulating through the region.

In Appalachia, educational opportunities are limited. Few students attend college, and if they do go, they often to do not graduate. The ARC (2010) reports that for most of the Appalachian core, only "4.9% to 11.5%"

of those living in the region have completed college. The monopolizing nature of large industries like the coal industry in the area has limited the growth of other types of work. This leads to a situation in which, as Altbach (1971) writes, modernization is hindered. The educational systems in these areas too often prepare students to simply enter the local workforce. This is problematic for much of Appalachia because in areas where one industry dominates (e.g., coal mines), that industry reaps most of the benefits from this labor, not the local community. Schools in these areas could improve this situation by preparing their students for more than local, manual labor and most importantly, helping these students become more aware and critical of their history, identity, and local surroundings. This type of instruction could create the "socially aware individuals needed for social and economic development" (Altbach, 1971).

Although the initial picture we have painted of Appalachia here seems rather bleak, there is much hope. Social justice has been a concern of many throughout the region. This is true because there have always been attitudes and actions of resistance in the region. As long as there has been coal company oppression, there has also been coal company resistance. We see examples of such action with the Blair Mountain labor uprising of the early 20th century and citizens' resistance to surface mining in their home areas. We are inspired by such acts of resistance, although we are calling for more resistance and action that centers in the classroom between student and teacher. Appalachia has been shaped by outsiders in government offices and boardrooms for far too long. We believe it is time that social justice is a systematic part of Appalachian education rather than a superficial piece of history that students have to seek outside the classroom to understand.

The concepts of place and identity are important in Appalachia, even though some in the region may not directly identify themselves with the region. For, like any identity, Appalachia is not only a physical construct, but it is a social one as well. One has to accept the construct to identify with it. For example, recently the concept of Appalachian identity was being discussed between members of a family. One of the family members mentioned that she had never really recognized herself as being "one of those people." This is an important observation pertaining to Appalachian identity, because many within the region have little collective consciousness about what it means to *be* Appalachian. Part of this may be because Appalachians are not often taught that they share some sort of positive collective identity with other Appalachians. Concerning instruction about their Appalachian identity, they may only remember being taught not to say "ain't" and other supposedly incorrect uses of English. The Appalachian identity is understandably denied when we see how the media generally represents Appalachians to those outside the region. Hollywood and other popular media sources are rampant with negative depictions of Appalachians. Examples of this are well documented, but some are movies like *Deliverance* and *Wrong Turn* and television shows like *Hee-Haw* and *The Beverly Hillbillies* (Williams, 2002). Appalachians, and outsiders to the region, only see themselves depicted as backwoods, ignorant, naïve, inbred, and unclean. It is no wonder that Appalachians do not want to identify with their own people.

The educational system within Appalachia has the responsibility to help students gain a more positive understanding of their own importance within the United States. Williams (2002) notes an interesting phenomenon pertaining to identity when he discusses historical depictions of Appalachians and their homeland. In earlier media discussions of the region and its people, Appalachia was described as a treacherous place, but one where the people were keen to own their land and always willing to come to the aid of travelers coming to and through the region. Once coal and other valuable minerals were discovered in the mountains, popular media began to change its tune. Suddenly, media outlets began describing Appalachians as savage people, always fighting in their drunkenness. Of course, scholars familiar with postcolonial theory will surely find the depiction of locals in a potentially economically wealthy region to be of no surprise. Appalachians were no longer portrayed as the intelligent, resourceful people they had been. Now that the land was to be exploited, it was necessary for the people and their identities to be exploited for the gain of large national corporations such as railroads, coal companies, and other ventures. Although this shift in perception of Appalachians is largely negative in present times, the fluidity of identity means that Appalachians can gain back positive depictions of their own identities via their own internal resources such as art, music, and education.

Further hope for the region resides in the fact that Appalachians are a notoriously resourceful people. As mentioned above, Appalachians' resistance to exploitation, although not part of the general regional identity, still remains influential in present times. In the last 100 years, Appalachians have collectively opposed labor inequities by going on strike for better working conditions in mines and hospitals, among other industries (Banks, 1999; Maggard, 1999). With this chapter, we hope to suggest some ways in which students and teachers can resist negative depictions from outsiders, gain a new collective Appalachian identity, and gain a richer educational experience that will highlight the region's uniqueness and importance to the United States. In many ways, Appalachians have shaped the very identity that outsiders understand to be uniquely a positive U.S. identity. Appalachians have played a pivotal role in modern U.S. culture and history (Biggers, 2006). We are calling for a collective Appalachian initiative to make these facts known and enjoyed by the very people who were responsible. We want young Appalachian children to recognize themselves as Appalachians and be proud to do so.

Along with identity, place is an important aspect of Appalachia that needs to be explored in a curriculum of the area. Appalachia is a pluralist region, one with many of its own contradictions and idiosyncrasies. Historically, some Appalachian states were Union, Southern, or neutral during the Civil War. Some states held slaves and others did not. There are large urban areas in the region and small towns scattered throughout. The importance of place within smaller sections of the greater Appalachian region becomes evident when considering a curriculum based on local identity and history.

In his discussion of a place-based pedagogy in the South, William Pinar (1991) mentions that Southern history is important in part because of its history with race relations and the Civil War (p. 166). The history of race and the Civil War is important in Appalachia due especially to the fact that, as mentioned above, Appalachia is a heterogeneous region. This is important because, unlike a strict Southern curriculum, Appalachia is both Northern and Southern in its entirety. There were free and enslaved African Americans throughout the general area of Appalachia. This is one of the many contradictions that a study of place can bring to the forefront for teachers and students of the region. The authors' own upbringing in both West Virginia and eastern Kentucky have brought about very real local contradictions with race and the Civil War. It is not uncommon for people in these regions, for example, to fly the Confederate flag, even though they themselves live in areas that were Northern and neutral, respectively. A curriculum of place that considers local contexts can bring up these seeming contradictions for students to consider their present and past from a more critical perspective.

In Appalachia, the most educated residents are often teachers. Even in very rural areas, there are often teachers who have completed master's degrees in their respective content areas. Although few teachers would like to be told they have even more responsibilities on their shoulders, they are uniquely positioned to serve as agents of change in their local communities. In the age of high-stakes, standardized testing, this may also be refreshing to teachers who feel all they do is teach to a test and have no control over their own curriculum. Most people agree that knowledge and education are powerful, and teachers are perfectly situated to make the young people in their classrooms both aware and critical of the discourses around them—discourses that they construct and are constructed within. The question is, how can such critical language awareness in students be cultivated?

In order to foster critical awareness of language and culture in students, we propose that teachers adopt a "trinocular framework"(Martin & Rose, 2007, p. 318), which will shape both classroom curriculum and classroom interaction. The trinocular framework presented by Martin and Rose (2007) is composed of three interrelated parts: logogenesis, ontogenesis, and phylogenesis. Logogenesis refers to a speaker's "instantiation of the text" (p. 318) in her own local context. In other words, it encompasses the "unfolding" (p. 318) of all the spoken and written texts that we create in our everyday life. Ontogenesis refers to the "development of the individual" (p. 318)—for example, who they are and what they do. Finally, phylogenesis refers to the "expansion of the culture" (p. 318)—for example, what a culture is currently like, how it has evolved, and where it might be going. Taken together, these three parts of the framework provide a view of the close relationship between language and culture:

> Where a culture has arrived in its evolution provides the social context for the linguistic development of the individual, and the point an individual is at in their development provides resources for the instantiation of unfolding texts . . . logogenesis provides the material (i.e., semiotic goods) for ontogenesis, which in turn provides the material for phylogenesis; in other words, texts provide the means through which individuals interact to learn the system. And it is through the heteroglossic aggregation of individual systems (that are always already social systems), through the changing voices of us all, that the semiotic trajectory of a culture evolves. (p. 318)

With this model in mind, we suggest a curriculum for Appalachia composed of critical reading of key Appalachian texts in order for students to learn more about their history and the nature of the culture around them (ontogenesis), student writing that is phenomenological and autobiographical (logogenesis)—giving students the chance to discover, articulate, and possibly rearticulate their own identities—and service-learning activities in which students identify and take action against problems in their local contexts (phylogenesis) and thereby effect change in the development and direction of their local culture.

We agree with the assertion in Hanley (2010) that the arts have the potential to "help students become metacognitive about their capacity for imagination, creativity, conceptualization, and transformation" (p. 191). Therefore, when choosing books for the ontogenesis part of the curriculum, it is important that teachers are careful and purposeful in their selection. The ideal book is not only well written, it reveals something new to students about their own histories and identities as residents of Appalachia. Such literature takes a complex and at times critical look at the region and the events that make up its history. Because the kinds of oppression that Appalachians face today are similar (if not identical) to those faced in the past, great literature about the region can be a powerful way to teach students about themselves. For example, many books set in the central Appalachian region take place in coal camps and tell of abuses of the land and people there. Although coal camps no longer exist, many of the communities initially formed as coal camps still remain. Perhaps even sadder are those coal camps that no longer exist—where the coal companies came in, exploited the people and the land, and once the coal was gone, moved on to establish their next company camp.

In *Storming Heaven* (1987) and its sequel, *The Unquiet Earth* (1992), Denise Giardina chronicles nearly a century of coal industry abuse and exploitation. Each of these remarkable books ends with a tragic event in Appalachian history. The events in *Storming Heaven* lead up to the battle of Blair Mountain, where a militia of 10,000 pro-union miners were attacked with firearms, bombs, and poison gas. *The Unquiet Earth* ends with the Buffalo Creek disaster. In 1972 in the Buffalo Creek valley of Logan County West Virginia, an earthen dam on Buffalo Creek burst and

> unleashed over 130 million gallons of water and waste materials—stream water from recent rains as well as black coal-waste water and sludge from a coal-washing operation. This 20-to-30-foot tidal wave of rampaging water and sludge, sometimes traveling at speeds up to 30 miles per hour, devastated Buffalo Creek's sixteen small communities. Over 125 people perished immediately. Most were women and children unable to struggle out from under the thick black water choked with crushed and splintered homes, cars, telephone poles, railroad tracks, and all manner of other debris. There were over 4,000 survivors, but their 1,000 homes were destroyed as well as most of their possessions. (Stern, 1976, pp. ix–x)

Both of these events are equally shocking and tragic, and surprisingly, largely forgotten about, even by those who live in this region. Books such as these are ideal for fostering a critical awareness of history and identity in Appalachian students. As students read and discuss the places, characters, and events in these works and begin to see pieces of themselves—and their lived experiences—in them, they will begin to experience an opening or awakening of self. As they begin to see themselves in a new way, they will begin to see their local community in a new way as well. Readings such as this provide students with the opportunity to view one another as a collective community with a collective history rather than just a class of many individuals.

When this new awareness of self begins growing, it is time to move to the logogenesis phase of the curriculum. In this phase, students will write about their own identities and their communities. Ideally, this writing will be autobiographical, phenomenological, or a combination of both. These writings will allow students to develop and further refine their understanding of their identity and local context. In addition, there are at least two more important benefits to this type of writing. The students will learn to resist the stereotypes about themselves and their region—many of which are internalized and naturalized—and redefine themselves on their own terms. Also, this type of writing can make oppression and the sources of oppression visible. Things like rampant poverty, which seem like a natural part of life, are seen in a new light—as oppression, as exploitation, as abuse.

These revelations are a key part of this curriculum because they are the impetus that leads to action in the local context—the phylogenesis phase of the curriculum. As students write and uncover problems in their school and community, they can begin to imagine ways to address them. These ideas could be shared among teachers and students within a classroom and lead to a service-learning project that seeks to improve a real need in the community. This social justice-focused curriculum equips students in Appalachia to identify the real needs of their communities and to work on solutions that address those needs. For these solutions to be viable, it is essential that they are created by the teachers and students of the region for their own local community. These solutions must be something that local communities can live with, and they must remake Appalachian communities into what local citizens want their Appalachia to become. For too many years, Appalachia, its people, and it's communities have been externally defined and controlled. Through the use of a critical curriculum, such as the one we have suggested, Appalachians can begin to take back control of their histories and identities. As students and teachers absorb and draw upon the many problematic texts in their communities and refract them through their own, more hopeful, lenses, they begin to simultaneously redefine and change the direction of Appalachian culture for future generations.

APPENDIX

The following are some suggested literature pairings. Each literary work listed corresponds to a disaster or form of oppression in Appalachia.

"Storming Heaven" (1987), Denise Giardina—Battle of Blair Mountain
"The Unquiet Earth" (1992), Denise Giardina—Buffalo Creek disaster
"River of Earth" (1978), James Still—coal camp/industry; poverty
"The Book of the Dead" in *U.S. 1* (1938), Muriel Rukeyser—Hawk's Nest
    Tunnel disaster
"Night Comes to the Cumberlands" (1962), Harry Caudill—Cumber-
    land region poverty
"Kettle Bottom" (2004), Diane Gilliam Fisher—coal camp life; poverty;
    battle of Blair mountain
"Coal: A Poetry Anthology" (2006), edited by Chris Green—coal camps;
    region; industry; people; etc.
"Raising the Dead" (2002), Ron Rash—Tennessee Valley Authority hy-
    droelectric power.

REFERENCES

Achinstein, B., & Athanases, S. Z. (2010). New teacher induction and mentoring for educational change. In A. Hargreaves, A. Lieberman, M. Fullan, & D. Hopkins (Eds.), *Second international handbook of educational change* (Vol. 23, pp. 573–593). The Netherlands: Springer.

Altbach, P. G. (1971). Education and neocolonialism. *Teachers College Record, 72*(1).

Appalachian Regional Commission. (2010, March). *Socioeconomic overview of Appalachia.* Retrieved from http://www.arc.gov/images/appregion/SocioeconomicOverviewofAppalachiaMarch2010.pdf

Ayers, W. (2004). *Teaching toward freedom.* Boston, MA: Beacon.

Banks, A. (1999). Miners talk back: Labor activism in southeastern Kentucky in 1922. In D. B. Billings, G. Norman, & K. Ledford (Eds.), *Back talk from Appalachia: Confronting stereotypes* (pp. 215–227). Lexington: University of Kentucky Press.

Biggers, J. (2006). *The United States of Appalachia: How Southern mountaineers brought independence, culture, and enlightenment to America.* Emeryville, CA: Shoemaker & Hoard.

Caudill, H. (1962). *Night comes to the Cumberlands.* Boston, MA: Little, Brown and Company.

Fisher, D. G. (2004). *Kettle bottom.* Florence, MA: Perugia Press.

Giardina, D. (1987). *Storming heaven.* New York, NY: Ivy.

Giardina, D. (1992). *The unquiet earth.* New York, NY: Ivy.

Green, C. (Ed.). (2006). *Coal: A poetry anthology.* Frankfort, KY: Blair Mountain Press.

Hanley, M. S. (2010). The arts and social justice in a critical multicultural education classroom. In S. May & C. E. Sleeter (Eds.), *Critical multiculturalism: Theory and practice* (pp. 191–201). New York, NY: Routledge.

Maggard, S. W. (1999). Coalfield women making history. In D. B. Billings, G. Norman, & K. Ledford (Eds.), *Back talk from Appalachia: Confronting stereotypes* (pp. 228–250). Lexington: University of Kentucky Press.

Martin, J., & Rose, D. (2007). *Working with discourse: Meaning beyond the clause* (2nd ed., p. 318). London, UK: Continuum.

National Center for Education Statistics (NCES). (2009). *The nation's report card. Reading 2009: National assessment of educational progress at grades 4 and 8* (NCES 2010-458). Washington, DC: Institute of Education Sciences, U.S. Department of Education. Retrieved from nces.ed.gov/nationsreportcard/reading

Pinar, W. F. (1991). Curriculum as social psychoanalysis: On the significance of place. In J. L. Kincheloe & W. F. Pinar (Eds.), *Curriculum as social psychoanalysis: The significance of place* (pp. 165–186). Albany, NY: SUNY Press.

Rash, R. (2002). *Raising the dead.* Oak Ridge, TN: Iris Press.

Rukeyser, M. (1938). *U.S. 1.* New York, NY: Covici-Friede.

Stern, G. M. (1976). *The Buffalo Creek disaster.* New York, NY: Vintage.

Still, J. (1978). *River of earth.* Lexington, KY: The University Press of Kentucky.

Williams, J. A. (2002). *Appalachia: A history.* Chapel Hill, NC: University of North Carolina Press.

Villegas, A. M., & Lucas, T. (2002). Preparing culturally responsive teachers: Rethinking the curriculum. *Journal of Teacher Education, 53*(1), 20–32.

Zeichner, K. M. (2009). *Teacher education and the struggle for social justice.* New York, NY: Routledge.

CHAPTER 8

AL OTRO LADO DEL PUENTE

Fostering Literacy Partnerships Between Academia and Latino/a Communities

Zaira R. Arvelo Alicea and Ileana Cortés Santiago

In this chapter, we describe our experiences working with Latino/a families and prospective teachers in the development and implementation of a small-scale community engagement project sponsored by a university-based grant. The main goal of this project is to highlight the importance of preparing prospective teachers to serve as agents in Latino/a children's literacy development. First, we discuss our involvement in this project as foregrounded by our experiences growing up in a Latino/a community in the Caribbean and our current research foci as doctoral students. Second, we present a model for promoting literacy development based on the remarkable work carried out by a Puerto Rican social agent. Then, we explain the conception of social justice that undergirds this project, which focuses on two tenets: family involvement and culturally sensitive curricula. Finally, we offer brief accounts of the events carried out in two venues to elucidate the implementation of our proposed literacy development model and our conception of social justice.

Teacher Education for Social Justice: Perspectives and Lessons Learned, pages 91–104.
Copyright © 2013 by Information Age Publishing
91

Zaira's Voice

As instructor of a teacher education course on children's and young adult literature, I constantly search for trade books that portray an accurate representation of the pluralistic experiences of Latinos/as who reside in the Caribbean, Latin America, and the United States. It was through this endeavor that the initial idea for our community engagement project materialized. While I perused local large bookstores, I realized that Latino/a literature for children was largely absent. The bookstores had areas dedicated to various addressee groups (e.g., boys' books), genres (e.g., fiction novels), reading levels, and even literary awards. Nonetheless, major Latino/a literature awards such as the Pura Belpré Award, granted by the American Library Association, and the Américas Book Award, given by the National Consortium of Latin American Studies Programs at the University of Wisconsin-Milwaukee, were nowhere to be found. As a result, I wondered how children and their families would learn about Latino/a literature and these awards when they were not featured in the bookstores as awards honoring Anglo European men such as the Newbery Medal and the Caldecott Medal. What possibility did Latino/a children's literature have if "the Newbery and Caldecott Medals, named after historic British innovators, canonize[d] newly published titles" (op de Beeck, 2010, p. 15)?

My experience visiting a local library was very similar to the aforementioned occurrences in the large bookstores. The information desks had brochures on the Newbery and the Caldecott Medals but did not have any information on Latino/a children's literature awards. One key feature of these brochures was a chronological listing of all the titles that had earned the award, along with their corresponding location in the library shelves. As Ewers (2009) explains, in their evaluative and distributive function, libraries make a range of books available by using "special lists and themed leaflets" (p. 68). Such distributive strategies are indicative of the literatures that are endorsed by library systems and the message that such endorsement disseminates to its users. In light of this, I pondered on issues of accessibility to meaningful texts: Why are decades of a group's quality literature given center stage while others are relegated to marginal spaces? How does such censorship render a culture's literature invisible and thus underrepresented? As I entertained these questions, I recalled my childhood experiences growing up, unable to find a book with characters that resembled my physiological features, lived on a tropical island, and spoke Spanish.

I completed my elementary education in a small school in a rural town in Puerto Rico, a school without a main building, where classrooms blended with the earth and the large trees surrounding them. Such a school also had its limitations: our school library consisted of a large classroom cluttered with ceiling-high old bookshelves without air conditioning in an ever-tropical weather. Still, I would venture into this musty room looking for books to take home and delve into my passion, one that was not shared by my family members, reading. The only time for stories occurred before bedtime, when *mami* would come to my room, which I shared with my older brother, and tell us stories that she had created or heard. Our house never had a bookshelf. I particularly remember a day when a sales representative went house by house selling encyclopedias, and my parents bought a set. With this set came an accompanying collection of children's books, which, although written in English, were the most beautiful books I had ever seen: a Dr. Seuss collection. One day, something changed; I arrived home, and the books were gone. *Mami* told me the sales representative had come back to collect, and she could not afford them.

It was precisely these childhood experiences, when reading was enjoyable yet difficult to achieve, that prompted me to develop a project focused on making meaningful literature accessible to Latino/a children in this Midwest university town. This initial idea would be further developed through the establishment of a continuing collaboration with a fellow Puerto Rican and doctoral student whose childhood experiences and research interests would reaffirm and extend my own.

Ileana's Voice

My great-grandmother used to read the letters of members of the community who could not read. Many of them were local agricultural workers who earned meager salaries in the nearby plantations. Others were farmers who cultivated tobacco and locally grown fruits and root vegetables to sustain their families. These people would gather around my stubborn *abuela* and listen to the words of their loved ones through her voice. Her letter-reading circles, in addition to her praying of the *rosario*, were thus education for those who listened and were lured by her sharing, my mother included. As a Caribbean woman, I have inherited an understanding of the organic nature of oral tradition and its transformative power to shape community literacies through strong female agents like my grandmother. In fact, my mother's recollection of *abuela's* strong presence as woman, parent, and educator for neighbors and friends served as constant reminder of what I had witnessed as a young child. This link between female agency in education and oral tradition has been central to Latino/a literacy development on the Island and among diasporic Puerto Ricans for decades [as also highlighted in Hernández-Delgado (1992)].

During childhood, *abuela* would tell me that on the eve of economic changes, when agrarian economies were substituted by industrialism, Puerto Ricans began journeys to the United States (see Pérez, 2004), carrying the value of storytelling and oral tradition with them. Upon arrival, employment and schooling became critical aspects that the Puerto Rican community had to address in order to improve their conditions (Nieto, 1995; Ranzal, 1947). As time passed, labels such as "problem" and "outsiders" were unjustly conferred on them in multiple printed media, such as *The New York Times*—a practice that caused major wounds on the collective perception of Puerto Rican identity (Nieto, 1995). As I ventured into the archives of *The New York Times* for printed media representations of Puerto Ricans in the neighborhoods, a concern emerged: that the schooling of my community was covered by a bitter mantle of discrimination that segregated families from the education provided by the State.

While peeling away layers of information that linked the newcomers from the Island to a ghetto (Cordasco, 1967) in which schools prepared minorities for the workforce, I was lured by the work of a network of women who were educating "against the grain," as Cochran-Smith puts it (2004, p. 24). One of those women was Pura T. Belpré, a Puerto Rican writer, community agent, librarian, and folklorist who developed a dynamic approach to community partnerships that allowed her to situate and disseminate literacy practices in both academic venues (i.e., libraries, schools) and community venues (i.e., homes, *plazas*, community centers). As I read available sources documenting the life of this commendable woman (Hernández-Delgado, 1992; Ortiz, 1990), I discovered that she journeyed the tempestuous waters of linguistic and cultural segregation, determined to offer communities a quality education; she achieved this by bringing novel and meaningful practices such as bilingual activities and folkloric elements to the Latinos/as in New York. Moreover, she became actively involved with families living in a system and context that was unknown to them. The figure of Belpré, as she was known to Zaira, a storyteller whose work would become exemplary of authentic Latino/a literature for children, and to me, a pioneer community agent, would become the model for literacy development and engagement that would eventually undergird our project.

OUR PURA T. BELPRÉ MODEL

Hernández-Delgado (1992) documented Belpré's insight as a concerned librarian who had noticed the lack of Latino/a presence in the New York Public Library. In one of her unpublished papers, Belpré (n.d.) emphasized the need to formally invite and guide families through a seemingly unknown system, the library. This invitation, along with her multiple outreach efforts, shows Belpré's commitment to designing cultural programs for the families. Through these events, she explained that Latino/a families were enriched, as they established connections with a story or a book that tapped into their experiences (see Belpré, n.d.). The comprehensive nature of her initiatives in New York served as a framework to conceptualize our literacy development model and approach the Latinos/as in our community with authentic literature and singing games responsive to their identities and needs. The model is informed by Belpré's efforts to partner and interact with community members in their geographical space, while creating an environment conducive to formative experiences. In her fluid movements between academic and community venues, she created spaces for literacy development, as shown in Figure 1. The hexagon shapes in the model represent what we have labeled *spaces for literacy development*, that is, unexpected moments and traditional places in which literacy events take place.

Hernández-Delgado (1992) documents the words of Daniel Chavez, a colleague of Belpré, who shared one such moment when literacy development took place amidst academic and community venues—in the interregnum:

> Having finished a story hour, [Belpré] was approached by a child and her grandmother outside the library. Since the child had arrived late for the story session, she asked if Belpré could recite a story for her grandmother. Despite being late for her next assignment, *Belpre happily told them a Puerto Rican folk tale, between two parked cars while the traffic whizzed by* [italics added]. Tears rolled down the grandmother's cheeks as the familiar tale was relived. (p. 434)

For Belpré, literacy development fluctuated across spaces, took multiple forms (i.e., oral, scribal, performance), and elicited myriad responses from the community. According to Ortiz (1990), this advocate worked with community engagement activities to foster language awareness and showcase the richness of Latino/a folklore by opening the door to families and commuting to the most remote corners of the neighborhoods. As explained by Hernández-Delgado (1992) in his recollection of an interview done to the storyteller, "Pura Belpré eagerly visited churches, community centers and neighborhood organizations and schools that desired cultural programs and library services" (p. 430); thus she created story time, book clubs, and bilingual story hours for underrepresented children and their families in traditional and alternative spaces. The allure of her events and activities most likely resided in her capacity to employ authentic stories that resonated with her audience and made them participants rather than recipients of knowledge. Belpré brought the colors, faces, and voices of Latinos/ as to the "cultural *ambiente* or ambience" of New York by building bridges between the library and the people in the neighborhoods (Ortiz, 1990, p. 43). It appears that she embraced community engagement as key in the development of meaningful experiences to better the education of children. Had it not been for these alternate forms of instruction in the city, perhaps these underrepresented groups might have been left to roam around the streets as truants of the school system—their families blamed for this systemic marginalization.

Geographical Space

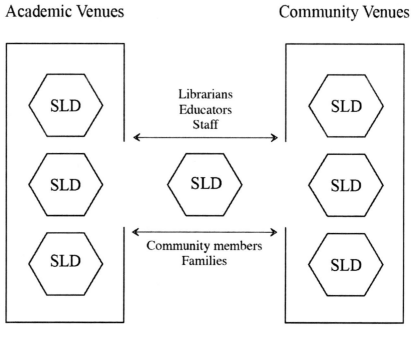

= spaces for literacy development

FIGURE 1.   Model for literacy development inspired by Pura T. Belpré's life and work.

SOCIAL JUSTICE PARADIGM

Migration and demographic change are ongoing, inevitable processes. According to the U.S. Census Bureau (2010a), 16.3% of people living in the United States and Puerto Rico identified themselves as Hispanic or Latino—a 43% increase in the nation. Large waves of Latinos/as have migrated to the United States for centuries, most of whom had previously settled in areas such as Texas, California, and New York but are now present in other regions, such as the Midwest. Ethnographic studies on Latinos/as in the states of Indiana, Michigan, and Ohio explain that these groups migrate in "quest for jobs and a better life" and ultimately settle for meager salaries in the food processing industry and agriculture available in the local economy

(Millard & Chapa, 2004, p. 6). This tendency creates the conditions that entangle them in a cycle of poverty, affecting their opportunities for quality education.

Migration patterns in Tippecanoe, Indiana, the county where this project took place, are consistent with the national demographic trend. In fact, Tippecanoe is one of seven counties with the largest demographic changes according to census data. Still, Hispanics or Latinos, as a group, comprise only a 6% of Indiana's population, whereas Whites represent 84.3% (U.S. Census Bureau, 2010b). This disparity materializes in a geographical mark—a river—which segregates this community while localizing them to specific spaces in our county. On the left side of the river, one can find the presence of a large university, with its student population, administrative staff, and professorate. On the right side, and past the downtown area, one can drive through a series of blocks displaying signs for Mexican bakeries, grocery stores, restaurants, and shops claiming *se habla español*. It is in this manner that a number or a percentage reported by the U.S. Census Bureau transforms into a cultural presence that creolizes what has traditionally been a homogenous setting. As educators, we are bound to ask the following question: How can a critical understanding of these demographic changes and localized presence, outside the college area, inform the preparation of our teachers? The answer: Schools cannot exist in isolation; as social institutions, they mimic the changes that occur beyond their walls and thus must be responsive to the educational needs of the communities they serve. Here, prospective and practicing teachers play a prominent role.

Family Involvement

Working with diverse families demands the unpacking of our traditional conception of nuclear family, which centers on the presence of a biological mother and father (Turner-Vorbeck, 2005). Latinos/as challenge this definition of family by integrating community members and nonnuclear family into their immediate circle. This is one reason for our choice to employ the term *family involvement* over the most commonly used term, *parental involvement* (Delgado-Gaitan, 2004, 2007). An understanding of Latino/a family values, coupled with an awareness of their socioeconomic conditions, provides us with the knowledge to question and break away from negative stereotypes. As Turner-Vorbeck (2008) explains, "Teachers commonly are quick to blame a student's poor academic achievement or slow social development on a substandard form of family rather than to explore their own pedagogy" (p. 185).

Although it would be easy to attribute the responsibility for lack of family involvement to labels of Latino/a families as low-income groups or immigrants who resist learning English, current research shows a different reality (Delgado-Gaitan, 2007). One factor that deters family involvement is the disconnect between home and school, especially through the means used for communication. In her study on parent's perceptions of their involvement in schools, Snell (2011) argues that Latino/a and African American parents feel confused about the institutions' rules and policies. As Bernhard (2010) explains, in her study of Latino/a parents in Canadian schools, parents felt that the teachers' language "left them feeling unable to make their views known . . . .The jargon and specialized terms that educators used during meetings such as *withdrawal, special education, below grade level functioning in English,* and *reading clinic* were not understood even when translators were employed" (p. 327). Lack of access to the discourses and technical terms often employed by teachers and administrators serves to diminish Latino/a families' disposition to join invitations for family-teacher communication and thickens the barriers between them.

As Latina educators, we understand that Latino/a families' concept of education might differ from the dominant ideal, which focuses mainly on academic formation. In a study on parental perceptions of educational involvement conducted using focus groups in Miami, New York, and Los Angeles, Zarate (2007) argues that parents perceive academic involvement and life participation as two different yet complementary categories that contribute to their children's education. She explains that, "Educación, as discussed in Latino families is different from education in that it encompasses social and ethical education, in addition to formal education. Educación is a holistic approach to learning and personal improvement" (p. 9). Such divergent definitions prompt Latino/a families to consider schools as "a province of teachers," who are experts in their subject areas (Levinson, Bucher, Harvey, Martínez, Pérez, Skiba, Harris, Cowan, & Chung, 2007, p. 15). *Educación* rather than academic formation is the area in which Latino parents participate the most. As Bernhard (2010) so aptly puts it, "What teachers call immigrant parents' lack of motivation and interest can be said to be an expression of the dynamic of their devaluation" (p. 324) because they engage in ways the school does not recognize. Thus, any teacher preparation program aiming to reach Latino/a families must prepare prospective teachers to understand what these communities value as education, in addition to modeling strategies for effective communication between the children's home and school.

Culturally Sensitive Curriculum

Banks (2003) explains that as nations, like the United States, continue to expand their "ethnic texture" (p. 19), schools need to prepare pupils to develop multicultural literacy, that is, the ability to see knowledge from multiple perspectives and the capacity to use this knowledge to enact change in the world. As stated by the American Association of Colleges for Teacher Education (1972), "Schools and colleges must assure that their total educational process and educational content reflect a commitment to cultural pluralism" (para. 8). One way in which educators can give voice to various perspectives in their classrooms is by developing curricula that incorporates authentic children's literature. As explained by Fox (2006), "Instructors who teach from a social justice perspective often use children's literature as the gateway" (p. 251). As a matter of fact, there is a need to develop a culturally sensitive curricula that affirms Latino/a children's identity and promotes an understanding of their cultural values.

A factor that prevents educators from seeing the need to enact curriculum changes is the widely acknowledged demographic gap between students and educators, who continue to be predominantly White (Sleeter, 2008). In an examination of English language arts teachers' selection of texts, Bender-Slack (2007) reports that the majority of the participants were complacent with using canonical texts; they considered the texts to be "timeless" and believed that social justice is a matter of how the texts are taught (p. 150). Such positioning, as Henderson (2005) explains, denotes "a sentimentality toward a text, a feeling that suggests that because a text is old, or considered a classic, it can no longer harm" (p. 267). These beloved texts, whose content may seem alien to underrepresented students, are traditional curricula that most children, including Latinos/as, are exposed to in schools. As González (2009) explains in her analysis of children's literature from Latin America and the Caribbean, "Children's literature has a vital role to play as a repository for the forgotten, a reminder of difference and plurality, a reflection of local cultural identities, and a source of agency and imagination" (p. 4). As such, children's literature has a transformative quality educators can grasp to foster cross-cultural journeys for all students and promote climates of empowerment for Latino/a students.

THE COMMUNITY ENGAGEMENT PROJECT

Our Pura Belpré Model in Practice

The Pura Belpré model that we delineated earlier served as foundation for the development of our initiative. We began by identifying the aforementioned Latino/a community in Tippecanoe, Indiana, and extending to them a formal invitation to join our project, which took place in two venues: the first was community based, a center; the second was academic, a public library. For both events, we created the necessary conditions for an inviting cultural ambience. During the community event, we featured traditional music, enlivened by the notes of children's self-made musical instruments. In addition, bilingual singing games were coupled with the families' energy as they danced, clapped, and chorused to the rhythm of "Shake it Morena!" one of several traditional songs documented in Bernier-Grand's (2002) authentic picture book. In the library, the traditional academic venue transformed into a space for literacy development that resembled González's (2008) rendering of how Belpré appropriated the Caribbean festivity of Three Kings Day and brought it to New York. In our case, the community festivity was that of a genuine birthday celebration in Latin America inspired by a concept book. During the read aloud, children located cultural artifacts mentioned in the story that had been placed in the room. The children also lifted and displayed signs to provide a visual representation of the various numbers mentioned in the story. In this manner, traditional academic literacies such as structured read alouds become meaningful by evoking the families' oral tradition and their more kinesthetic responses to texts. For the birthday party portion of the event, the families sang birthday songs in English and Spanish and the traditional *Las Mañanitas*, a song akin to Mexican culture. They also popped a piñata as featured in the book. Finally, in light of the particularities of our community, the components of the model that were pertinent were extending a formal invitation, promoting new spaces for literacy development, and paying close attention to the details that turn a venue into a familiar and safe space.

Family Involvement in Practice

As educators, a main concern when developing this project was facilitating cross-cultural interactions between predominantly White preservice teachers and Latino/a families. Through both events, preservice teachers had to unpack various myths about Latino/a parents as disconnected from their children's literacy education. Some common notions we hoped to challenge were that (a) families discourage their children from using English, (b) they do not respond to invitations to educational events, and (c) they do not dialogue with teachers. Instead, prospective teachers witnessed Latino/a families undertaking active and responsive roles while partaking of the activities. During the first event, Latino/a families attended and engaged in a workshop delivered by a Latina professor. Families worked hand-in-hand with the facilitator and other community members to construct a collective image of what it means to be the parent of a Latino/a child in the United States (Delgado-Gaitan, 2004). This image was created through the sharing of testimonials that recounted experiences of migration, cultural marginalization, and linguistic segregation. During the library event, we observed how the Latino/a parents' role became that of facilitator and leader of small group projects. After they were provided with a creative license to aid their children in the creation of a mask, they undertook this indefinite project and made it a shared experience in which everyone's children received instruction from the parent-teachers. The common goal, creating a mask, served as a catalyst to learning, the breaking of personal spaces, and the allocation of roles. In this manner, a population that is traditionally underrepresented in these spaces had a protagonist's role.

Culturally Sensitive Literature in Practice

"Culturally sensitive" should be more than a trendy, politically correct gimmick commonly employed in scholarly work. It must be a pedagogical stance leading to curricular interventions that proclaim cultural and linguistic diversity as norm. In our project, we addressed the need for culturally sensitive materials by incorporating award winning Latino/a children's literature. The inclusion of these books served a dual function: it made preservice teachers cognizant of an alternative canon, one that celebrates the contributions of Latino/a authors and illustrators, and it also created a connection between families and formal literacies.

At the community center, the facilitator shared poems from Argueta's (2001) *A Movie in My Pillow/Una Película en mi Almohada*, an Américas Award winning book that narrates the experience of Jorgito, a child crossing into the United States. In response to the poems, a Latino male in his late-20s shared that his feelings of loss resembled Jorgito's, who had lost his dearest pet after leaving El Salvador. Accordingly, scholars in the field of children's literature have argued that literature can serve as a doorway for entering a difficult conversation through "the 'blurring' of story and life" (Sipe & Daley, 2005, p. 233). For this participant, the contentious issues at hand were those of loss and immigration. Thus, he carried out an exchange with the text in which the fictional character's parrot became the tangible pet that was left in Latin America during the crossing. Through the implementation of culturally sensitive literature, a safe space was created and culturally specific experiences were affirmed. It was through this process of voicing personal experiences that the distant yet often-heard topic of immigration was articulated as a local and latent human issue. For the second activity, we selected Morales's (2003) *Just a Minute: A Trickster Tale and Counting Book*, a Pura Belpré Award winner. The criteria that motivated the selection of this book was its display of authentic motifs characteristic of Latino/a literature for children, which include the use of cunning characters disguised as innocent or tricksters (González, 2009), dual language (Van Dongen, 2005), and an extended family. As the read aloud took place, children favored the witty *abuela* who constantly fooled her birthday guests.

FINAL THOUGHTS

We started this chapter by revisiting our literacy practices upon which we foregrounded our current engagement interest. With this common ground, we set goals to develop a model based on an outstanding community advocate who embodied best practices for reaching out to Latino/a communities. To do this successfully, we grounded this model in our current context, including location, sociodemographics, linguistic and cultural diversity, and the ongoing conversations on teacher preparation for social justice. This foundation allowed us to develop a project that fostered partnerships between academia and the community. Reflecting on the outcomes of this project, we offer our concluding remarks and recommendations.

First, our Pura Belpré Model as an action plan is not intended solely for reaching out to Latino/a communities; instead, it is offered as a dynamic concept that could be implemented in teacher preparation programs to guide prospective teachers in the service of underrepresented groups. You can take our model or identify a key figure in your community who embodies best literacy practices and develop your own. Second, our conception of family involvement is overarching, for it integrates extended family and community members and positions them as agents. Teacher preparation programs can share with students effective strategies to communicate with families in ways that promote equal participation, in which both parties have the opportunity to contribute to the conversation and engage actively. In this manner, teachers and families can identify shared goals and establish an action plan.

Third, a pluralistic curriculum should be the curriculum—period. There is no doubt we are a diverse nation; as such, we cannot endorse a curriculum that implies the existence of a homogenous one. We understand that pluralism as norm would require time and effort from educators already burdened by State mandates. For this reason, teacher preparation programs should aid students in the process of locating and identifying materials based on ideals of multiplicity and authenticity. Also, these programs have the responsibility to inculcate the value of collaboration among academic personnel such as librarians, language teachers, and English Language Learning (ELL) specialists. Not sharing the language of your students does not mean you are unable to develop effective bilingual lessons. Tap into your librarian's ability to locate books, your language teachers' skills to determine the accuracy of a text, and the ELL specialist's expertise to assess the reading level of materials. Do not deprive yourself of the opportunity to develop formative projects for all your students and partner with their families.

REFERENCES

American Association of Colleges for Teacher Education. (1972). *No one model American*. Washington, DC. Commission on Multicultural Education.

Argueta, J. (2001). *A movie in my pillow/Una película en mi almohada*. San Francisco, CA: Children's Book Press.

Banks, J. A. (2003). Teaching literacy for social justice and global citizenship. *Language Arts, 81*(1), 18–19.

Belpré, P. T. (n.d.). *Puerto Rican folklore: Report for NYPL. Puerto Rican writers and migration: Folklore, autobiography & history.* Centro de Estudios Puertorriqueños, Hunter College, NY.

Bender-Slack, D. A. (2007). *Teaching texts for social justice: English teachers as agents of change.* (Doctoral dissertation). (UMI No. 3280095). Cincinnati, OH: University of Cincinnati.

Bernhard, J. K. (2010). From theory to practice: Engaging immigrant parents in their children's education. *The Alberta Journal of Educational Research, 56*(3), 319–334.

Bernier-Grand, C. T. (2002). *Shake it, Morena! and other folklore from Puerto Rico.* Brookfield, CT: Millbrook.

Cochran-Smith, M. (2004) *Walking the road: Race, diversity, and social justice in teacher education.* New York, NY: Teachers College Press.

Cordasco, F. M. (1967). The Puerto Rican child in the American school. *Journal of Human Relations, 15*(4), 500–509.

Delgado-Gaitan, C. (2004). *Involving Latino families in schools.* Thousand Oaks, CA: Corwin.

Delgado-Gaitan, C. (2007). Fostering Latino parent involvement in the schools: Practices and partnerships. In S. J. Paik & H. J. Walberg (Eds.), *Narrowing the achievement gap strategies for educating Latino, Black, and Asian students* (pp. 17–32). New York, NY: Springer Science + Business Media.

Ewers, H. (2009). *Fundamental concepts of children's literature research: Literary and sociological approaches.* New York, NY: Routledge.

Fox, K. R. (2006). Using author studies in children's literature to explore social justice issues. *The Social Studies, 97*(6), 251–256.

González, L. (2008). *The storyteller's candle/La velita de los cuentos.* San Francisco, CA: Children's Book Press.

González, A. (2009). *Resistance and survival: Children's narrative from Central America and the Caribbean.* Tucson: University of Arizona Press.

Henderson, D. L. (2005). Authenticity and accuracy: The continuing debate. In. J. P. May & D. L. Henderson (Eds.), *Exploring culturally diverse literature for children and adolescents: Learning to listen in new ways* (pp. 266–276). Boston, MA: Allyn and Bacon.

Hernández-Delgado, J. L. (1992). Pura Teresa Belpré, storyteller and pioneer Puerto Rican librarian. *The Library Quarterly, 62*(4), 425–440.

Levinson, B. A. U., Bucher, K., Harvey, L., Martínez, R., Pérez, B., Skiba, R., Harris, B., Cowan, P., & Chung, C. G. (2007, August). *Latino language minority students in Indiana: Trends, conditions and challenges.* Center for Evaluation & Education Policy. Retrieved from http://ceep.indiana.edu/projects/PDF/Latino_Language_Minority_Students_Indiana.pdf

Millard, A. V. & Chapa, J. (2004). *Apple pie and enchiladas: Latino newcomers in the Midwest.* Austin: University of Texas Press.

Morales, Y. (2003). *Just a minute!: A trickster tale and counting book.* San Francisco, CA: Chronicle.

Nieto, S. (1995). A history of the education of Puerto Rican students in U.S. mainland schools: "Losers," "outsiders," or "leaders"? In J. A. Banks (Ed.), *Handbook of research on multicultural education* (pp. 388–411). New York, NY: Macmillan.

op de Beeck, N. (2010). *Suspended animation: Children's picture books and the fairy tale of modernity.* Minneapolis: University of Minnesota Press.

Ortíz, A. (1990). The lives of pioneras: Bibliographic and research sources on Puerto Rican women in the United States. *Centro Journal, 2*(7), 40–47.

Pérez, G. M. (2004). *The near Northwest side story: Migration, displacement, and Puerto Rican families.* Berkeley, CA: U of California.

Ranzal, E. (1947, February 23). *Puerto Rico Seeks to curb migration.* New York Times, 20.

Sipe, L. R., & Daley, P. A. (2005). Story-reading, story-making, story-telling: Urban African American kindergartners respond to culturally relevant picture books. In J. P. May & D. Henderson (Eds.), *Exploring culturally diverse literature for children and adolescents: Learning to listen in new ways* (pp. 229–242). Boston, MA: Allyn and Bacon.

Sleeter, C. E. (2008). Preparing White teachers for diverse students. In M. Cochran-Smith, S. Feiman-Nemser, J. McIntyre, & K. E. Demers (Eds.), *Handbook of teacher research on teacher education: Enduring questions in changing contexts* (pp. 559–582). New York, NY: Routledge.

Snell, P. (2011). Parents defining parent involvement. In C. Compton-Lilly & S. Greene (Eds.), *Bedtime stories and book reports: Connecting parent involvement and family literacy* (pp. 29–38). New York, NY: Teachers College Press.

Turner-Vorbeck, T. A. (2005). Expanding multicultural education to include family diversity. *Multicultural Education, 13*(2), 6–10.

Turner-Vorbeck, T. A. (2008). From textbooks to the teachers' lounge: The many curricula of family in schools. In T. A. Turner-Vorbeck & M. Miller Marsh (Eds.). *Other kinds of families: Embracing diversity in schools* (pp.178–191). New York, NY: Teachers College Press.

U.S. Census Bureau. (2010a). *Profile of national population.* Retrieved April 30, 2011, from http://2010.census.gov/2010census/data/

U.S. Census Bureau. (2010b). *State & county quickfacts: Indiana.* Retrieved April 30, 2011, from http://quickfacts.census.gov/qfd/states/18000.html

Van Dongen, R. (2005). Reading literature multiculturally: A stance to enhance reading of some Hispanic children's literature. In. J. P. May & D. L. Henderson (Eds.), *Exploring culturally diverse literature for children and adolescents: Learning to listen in new ways* (pp. 157–167). Boston, MA: Allyn and Bacon.

Zarate, M. E. (2007). Understanding Latino parental involvement in education: Perceptions, expectations, and recommendations. *The Tómas Rivera Policy Institute.* Retrieved from http://www.closingtheachievementgap.org/cs/ctag/download/resources/38/latino_parent_zarate.pdf?x-r=pcfile_d

CHAPTER 9

PREPARING MATHEMATICS TEACHERS FOR CULTURALLY AND LINGUISTICALLY DIVERSE STUDENTS

What's Language Got to Do With Social Justice?

David Norris and Luciana C. de Oliveira

Mathematics is sometimes referred to as a "gatekeeping" subject, because of the role it plays in students' furthering their education and entering a more highly technical workforce with strong mathematical demands (de Freitas, 2008).Thus, mathematics teachers can act as the "gatekeeper," either allowing them to enter a world in which opportunities are afforded by mathematics, or locking them out. This puts mathematics teachers in a unique position of power of which they may be unaware (de Freitas, 2008). So why are some students allowed passage through the gate while others are left to remain outside? Why is it that White, middle-class, English speaking students enter at a higher rate than their culturally and linguistically diverse counterparts, as evidenced in such things as mathematics achieve-

Teacher Education for Social Justice: Perspectives and Lessons Learned, pages 105–114.
Copyright © 2013 by Information Age Publishing

ment tests and students entering fields in science, technology, engineering and mathematics (STEM)?

This becomes of particular concern as classrooms in the United States become more culturally and linguistically diverse (de Oliveira & Athanases, 2007; Lucas, Villegas, & Freedson-Gonzalez, 2008; Milner, 2010; Villegas & Lucas, 2002). For example, according to the 2005 census, there were approximately 48 million English language learners (ELLs) in U.S. classrooms, an increase of almost 50% over a ten-year period(U.S. Census Bureau, 2005). Hoffert (2009) estimated that one in seven students speaks a language other than English at home. With this increase of culturally and linguistically diverse students (CLDs) in the classroom, it becomes vital that preservice mathematics teachers (PMTs) are prepared to meet the needs of these students and allow them to develop the skills and knowledge necessary to pass through the gate. The vast majority of PMTs in mathematics education preparation programs come from White, middle-class, English speaking backgrounds (Grant & Gillete, 2006; Milner, 2010; Murray, 2010). However, with the increasing presence of CLDs in mathematics classrooms, these PMTs will more than likely teach in classrooms with students who come from different cultural and linguistic backgrounds than their own (McDonald, 2005; Milner, 2010).

Many current teacher preparation programs include only one or two courses in multiculturalism, usually isolated from other coursework (McDonald, 2007; Murray, 2010; Sleeter, 2009; Villegas & Lucas, 2002). Within these courses, PMTs may be introduced to issues about language, but they contain no real methods to address them in practice (de Oliveira & Athanases, 2007). Even when these courses increase awareness of issues, they typically do not help the PMTs put any methods into practice (McDonald, 2005). Part of this problem may be perpetuated by the lack of diversity among mathematics educators and their inexperience with methods to teach CLDs (de Oliveira & Athanases, 2007; Grant & Gillette, 2006). Additionally, many mathematics education programs frontload methods and content classes, culminating in a short period of students teaching. In order to prepare PMTs to face the challenges and meet the needs of culturally and linguistically diverse classrooms, certain issues need to be brought to light.

PRECONCEIVED NOTIONS OF CLDS AND LANGUAGE

PMTs need to address and confront their preconceived ideas about CLDs. The first issue is a possible (even subconscious) stereotyping based on the CLDs' country of origin. In a survey given to PMTs by Chval & Pinnow (2010), the PMTs were asked what accommodations they would make for students in their classrooms from different countries. For students immigrating from Asia, many of the PMTs responded that they would need to "challenge" these students; on the other hand, many responded that students immigrating from Central America would require some type of remediation. Instead of looking at the students as individuals, they are viewing them from a biased perspective based on cultural stereotypes. CLDs need to be seen as heterogeneous, even if they have similar cultural and linguistic backgrounds (Schleppegrell, 2010).

Beyond country of origin is the issue of language. Mathematics is often misconstrued as a "universal language," and because of its multimodal nature and use of symbols, it can transcend language (Hoffert, 2009; Solano-Flores, 2010). For example, in most countries, the expression "3 + 5" carries the same meaning. The symbols "3" and "5" both denote quantities, and the "+" sign carries with it the idea of the process of addition. Therefore, in most countries, this expression is understood. However, what if the class was being taught in Polish and you needed to respond orally to give the solution to this problem? You know the answer is "8," but how to you express that in Polish (*osiem*)? This view of math as drawing less on language than other subjects has been debunked (de Oliveira 2012; Schleppegrell, 2010). Consider the following example. Suppose you were to enter a mathematics classroom with the following written on the blackboard: "Em uma chácara existem galinhas e coelhos totalizando 35 animais, os quais somam juntos 100 pés. Determine o número de galinhas e coelhos existentes nessa chácara." What are you being asked to perform? And even if you were to unpack the problem, would you have the language necessary to answer it? In any subject, including mathematics, language and learning cannot be separated (de Oliveira & Cheng, 2011; Fernandez, Anhalt, & Civil, 2009; Lucas et al., 2008). PMTs need to be aware that mathematics and language are innately intertwined.

Once PMTs have dispelled this myth about mathematics, they can realize that language proficiency does *not* equate to mathematical proficiency. They need to realize that when CLDs are tested in mathematics, the assessments are given in English, and thus not only are they tested on their mathematical proficiency, but also their English proficiency (Callahan, 2005; Solano-Flores, 2006). However, it is vitally important that CLDs are truly assessed in their academic proficiency so that they can be placed in the proper level of mathematics (Moschkovich, 1999). This is when the multimodality of mathematics can become useful. Many of the symbols used by mathematics are fairly universal (such as the number symbols to represent quantity and process symbols such as + and ×). Students can use these to communicate knowledge when they do not have the words to do so. Additionally, mathematics makes use of graphs, charts, diagrams, and such. When students are unable to say what they are trying to communicate, they can draw a representation to express their knowledge.

The inability to differentiate between language proficiency and academic proficiency can lead to a deficit view of CLDs. de Freitas (2008) found that PMTs often used a deficit model to explain the differences in achievement among different cultural groups. This can be dangerous, because again, language proficiency is being tied to academic proficiency. Instead, teachers need to be able to find out where and why the students are struggling (Chubbuck, 2010), and instead concentrate on teaching content over focusing on perceived deficits (Fernandez et al., 2009). One such issue arises in code-switching. This occurs when a student "slides" between two languages, either between or within sentences. Code-switching is often viewed as a deficit, as a way for students who do not have complete knowledge of English to fill in the gaps using their native tongue (Solano-Flores, 2010). However, it has been shown that this actually expresses a richer knowledge of language, as the syntactical forms from each language are preserved as utterances flow from one language to another.

Many of the preconceived notions with which PMTs enter the field of education may be subconscious in nature. Only by explicitly bringing these "hidden" ideas into the conscious can they confront these issues and create change. They need to be able to determine who their students really are, not who they perceive them to be. In addition, the role of language in mathematics learning needs to be taken into consideration.

THE LANGUAGE OF MATHEMATICS

Language is sociocultural in nature. Its uses and meaning are derived from who is using it, in what context, and for what purpose. Moschkovich (2010a) states,

> We all participate in using language and, thus, we have developed intuitions about language based on our personal experience. Our personal experiences with language are couched in complex social, political, and historical contexts, and our intuitions may have developed into language attitudes. (p. 2)

PMTs, having been exposed to the language of mathematics for a good portion of their lives, may not recognize the specialized and technical forms that the language of mathematics can take. They need to be aware of the difference between academic language and everyday language. Academic language is the kind of language students learn at school and is different from ordinary language for communicative purposes (Schleppegrell, 2001, 2004). Academic language is generally learned in school from teachers and textbooks, and only with proper instructional support (Fillmore & Snow, 2000; Schleppegrell, 2004). Academic language is used differently in each one of the content areas. For instance, mathematics has its own ways of meaning-making that make it different from history. PMTs should know that they need to foster the use of academic language in CLDs. Strict use of everyday language to communicate in mathematics may lead to or re-inforce misconceptions (Schleppegrell, 2007), and students need active use of mathematical language to communicate and derive mathematical meanings (Moschkovich, 2010a). Students need to be instructed in how to negotiate the academic language of mathematics and move from informal to more technical language (Schleppegrell, 2007).

CLDs need to be encouraged to develop and use the proper mathematics register. Simplifying language does little to create clarity of mathematical concepts and actually tends to obscure them (Schleppegrell, 2010). Additionally, by simplifying language, CLDs have limited access and exposure to academic language appropriate for use in different disciplines (Callahan, 2005). This is important because as mathematics becomes more advanced, it becomes more dependent upon language (Schleppegrell, 2007). Typically, if the language becomes "watered down," the mathematics, by its dependence on language, becomes less rigorous. As a result, it decreases mathematical learning and thus further distances these students from grade-appropriate material, as well as their advancement in mathematics (Callahan, 2005). Students are socialized in mathematical discourse via participation, thus it is particularly important for CLDs to participate in classroom discourse in developing their academic language as well as their mathematical thinking (K. D. Gutiérrez, Sengupta-Irving, & Dieckmann, 2010). If needed, teachers can rephrase or reword utterances made in informal everyday language to appropriate academic language (Fernandez et al., 2009; Schleppegrell, 2007).

Since use of the academic language of mathematics is important, PMTs need to be aware of the specifics of the mathematics register that must be made explicit. First is the vocabulary and grammar of mathematics. Mathematics has vocabulary that is unique to the subject, such as *hypotenuse* and *logarithm*, which must be learned explicitly. Yet it also borrows words from everyday language that take on new meanings within mathematics, such as *table* and *product*. CLDs, in particular ELLs, may need direct instruction on the new use of these words. In addition, mathematics often nominalizes processes, turning them into "things" (Schleppegrell, 2007). Take the word *subtraction*. Subtraction refers to a process, yet the language of mathematics has converted it into a noun. When teachers use the noun subtraction, they are referring to the process of subtraction. There are also instances in mathematics in which a word can be used as both a thing and a process. For example, in geometry, the word *square* refers to a geometric shape with all sides congruent and four right angles; in algebra, the word *square* refers to the process of multiplying a number by itself. These two uses can be connected (such as visually determining how to square 3 by drawing a 3×3 square), but in more abstract conditions, connections are usually not made.

Mathematics also contains some unique grammatical structures that may create difficulty. A typical problem in mathematics may be "John had

6 cookies. If he gave 2 away, how many did he have left?" This problem concludes with an *–if* clause and a question. In conversational English, *–if* statements are typically conditional, as in *–if* this is true, *–then* this is true. However, in mathematics, an *–if* structure generally indicates that what follows is a fact, and generally is a vital piece of information needed to solve the problem. A similar structure often seen in mathematics is something such as "let $x =$." Again, this statement might seem conditional, as if saying "x could possibly be this" when really a definition is being stated. CLDs who have not been introduced to this type of grammatical structure may need help in unpacking the meaning in the structure (See de Oliveira, 2012, for information about how to analyze word problems with CLDs).

Chval & Pinnow (2010) stated that some PMTs recommended direct translation as an accommodation for ELLs in mathematics classrooms. Whereas this may have some benefits, it is not always recommended (Moschkovich, 1999). One issue with this method is that ELLs need to learn appropriate mathematical language in English, since ultimately their mathematical proficiency will be tested in English (Solano-Flores, 2006). Additionally, one of the goals of learning mathematics is to learn a way of thinking and reasoning, therefore "emphasis should be on getting students to work in natural mathematics contexts (e.g., to explain mathematical problem solving) beyond mere translation of words" (R. Gutiérrez, 2002). Direct translations are not always feasible; for example, academic mathematical language may not be the same in Spanish as it is in English. Whatever language in which the mathematics is being learned, it needs to be learned in the academic register of that language. Schleppegrell (2007) contends that

> If teachers have not learned the mathematics register in the language of instruction, they may not be in a position to scaffold students' development of that register and the accompanying mathematical concepts. To use the mathematics register at the appropriate level of technicality, a bilingual educator needs to be bilingual in mathematics. (p. 154)

Consider the following example. The problem, "The legs of the right triangle have measures of five and twelve. What is the length of the hypotenuse?" translated into Portuguese is "Os lados do triangulo direito medem cinco e doze. Qual é o comprimento da hipotenusa?" However, the word for *leg* in Portuguese is *perna*, but in translating to the academic language necessary for academic meaning in Portuguese, it is translated as *lados*. Thus, direct translation is not recommended unless the teacher is fluent in the academic mathematical register of that language.

Arming PMTs with knowledge of the structures and peculiarities of mathematical language can prepare them to meet the needs of a linguistically diverse classroom. In understanding how the language of mathematics differs from everyday language, as well as the importance of appropriate register, they can identify issues and encourage rigorous mathematics and mathematical thinking for all students.

CULTURE AND MATHEMATICS

PMTs need to realize that CLDs' educational experiences are shaped by their home cultures, language, time in the United States, and other factors (de Oliveira & Athanases, 2007). In considering their students, they need to look at more than test scores and language proficiency. Home culture plays a large part in the shaping of a student's identity, and different social groups communicate within their own culture in different ways (K. D. Gutiérrez et al., 2010). Teachers need to see the world through their students' frames of references (Sleeter, 2009), and in order to do this, they need explicit knowledge of the students' home cultures (Gay, 2002; Sleeter, 2009). In this way, they can see what is valued in that community (Gay, 2002), and take this knowledge and use it to bridge home culture to that of school mathematics (K. D. Gutiérrez et al., 2010; Gutstein & Peterson, 2005; Villegas & Lucas, 2002).

In doing so, teachers can make mathematics more relevant to students' lives. K. D. Gutiérrez et al. (2010) discuss studies in which students were observed doing mathematics within their communities; however, when a mathematical algorithm was introduced in school, asking them to perform the same task, they had difficulty. Thus, they had the mathematical skills within their community, but it was somehow lost in the translation to the more formal world of schooling. In knowing the culture of the community, teachers can be co-creating sociomathematical norms in their classrooms and thereby encourage more independent mathematical discourse among students. In seeing that mathematics is embedded in cultural contexts, students can see "what it means to do mathematics" (p. 61). Additionally, "teachers can use childrens' cultural capital to stimulate mathematics learning or ignore it and actively deplete motivation to learn, thus adding another barrier to achievement" (Averill et al., 2009, p. 159).

Effective teachers have knowledge of and interact within their students' communities (Grant & Gillette, 2006). However, teachers typically have little knowledge of that community (Athanases & de Oliveira, 2010). This situation is further exacerbated for PMTs by their limited time doing fieldwork (Villegas & Lucas, 2002). With such a small window of time in the classroom, it is hard for them to gain experience and knowledge of their students' home cultures. McDonald (2005) calls for more actual experience with CLDs over methods classes, in which students sit and learn *how* to teach rather than actually *experiencing* it. But preservice teachers do not just need more time and experience in the classroom, they also need to be exposed to a variety of students and conditions (Grant & Gillette, 2006; Sleeter, 2009). In addition, these preservice teachers need good role models (Athanases & de Oliveira, 2010) as well as exposure and access to culturally responsive teachers (Milner, 2010).

LANGUAGE, MATHEMATICS, AND SOCIAL JUSTICE

Teacher education programs that emphasize social justice regard the preparation of teachers with the knowledge, dispositions, and practices to work with culturally and linguistically diverse students as a fundamental responsibility of teacher education. They have a common aim of preparing teachers to recognize, specify, and resist inequity in schools and society (Zeichner, 2009).This chapter emphasizes the need to prepare mathematics teachers for social justice, highlighting what kinds of knowledge and practices preservice mathematics teachers need in order to be prepared to work in culturally and linguistically diverse classrooms. They need to realize that these students are in their classroom and overcome preconceived ideas they may have about these students; they need to understand the role that language plays in mathematics and stress the use of academic language while supporting its development; they need to understand the frames of reference from which their students enter the classroom and use this to build mathematical discourse and thinking. How else can PMTs be prepared to meet the challenges and needs in a culturally and linguistically diverse classroom?

Moschkovich (2010b) offers four traits that will make a mathematics teacher successful: (a) a high commitment to students' academic success and to the student—home communication, (b) high expectations for all students, (c) the autonomy to change curriculum and instruction to meet the specific needs of their students, and (d) a rejection of models of their students as intellectually disadvantaged. Items (a) and (d) have previously been discussed in this chapter. High expectations were mentioned in the development and use of academic language; however, this also applies to the level of mathematics that students need to learn. When teachers see students struggling, they often want to lower their expectations (Milner, 2010), but they need to keep expectations high (Athanases & de Oliveira, 2010), because "when little is expected, little is produced" (Callahan, 2005, p. 311).

Teachers also need the freedom, ability, and willingness to adjust curriculum as needed to meet the needs of individual students. Each student is unique and brings unique experiences to the classroom. Teachers can take advantage of this by tailoring lessons around these experiences to create a shared experience upon which learning can be constructed.

By instilling these traits into PMTs, we can send them out with the ability to teach CLDs appropriate and rigorous mathematics, support their development of mathematics discourse and mathematical thinking, and empower them in their own learning. In this way, these PMTs are no longer gatekeepers, but instead are ushers guiding *all* students through the gate.

REFERENCES

Athanases, S. Z., & de Oliveira, L. C. (2010). Toward program-wide coherence in preparing teachers to teach and advocate for English language learners. In T. Lucas (Ed.), *Teacher preparation for linguistically diverse classrooms: A resource for teacher educators* (pp. 195–215). New York, NY: Routledge.

Averill, R., Anderson, D., Easton, H., Te Maro, P., Smith, D., & Hynds, A. (2009). Culturally responsive teaching of mathematics: Three models from linked studies. *Journal for Research in Mathematics Education, 40*(2), 157–186.

Callahan, R. M. (2005). Tracking and high school English learners: Limiting opportunity to learn. *American Educational Research Journal, 42*(2), 305–328.

Chubbuck, S. M. (2010). Individual and structural orientations in socially just teaching: Conceptualization, implementation, and collaborative effort. *Journal of Teacher Education, 61*(3), 197–210.

Chval, K. B., & Pinnow, R. J. (2010). Pre-service teachers' assumptions about Latino/a English language learners in mathematics. *Teaching for Excellence and Equity in Mathematics, 2*(1), 6–13.

de Freitas, E. (2008). Troubling teacher identity: Preparing mathematics teachers to teach for diversity. *Teaching Education, 19*(1), 43–55.

de Oliveira, L. C. (2012). The language demands of word problems for English language learners. In S. Celedón-Pattichis & N. Ramirez (Eds.), *Beyond good teaching: Advancing mathematics education for ELLs* (pp. 195–205). Reston, VA: National Council of Teachers of Mathematics.

de Oliveira, L. C., & Athanases, S. Z. (2007). Graduates' reports of advocating for English language learners. *Journal of Teacher Education, 58*(3), 202–215.

de Oliveira, L. C., & Cheng, D. (2011). Language and the multisemiotic nature of mathematics. *The Reading Matrix, 11*(3), 255–268.

Fernandez, A., Anhalt, C. O., & Civil, M. (2009). Mathematical interviews to assess Latino students. *Teaching Children Mathematics, 16*(3), 162–169.

Fillmore, L., & Snow, C. E. (2000). *What teachers need to know about language.* Washington, DC: Center for Applied Linguistics.

Gay, G. (2002). Preparing for culturally responsive teaching. *Journal of Teacher Education, 53*(2), 106–116.

Grant, C. A., & Gillette, M. (2006). A candid talk to teacher educators about effectively preparing teachers who can teach everyone's children. *Journal of Teacher Education, 57*(3), 292–299.

Gutiérrez, K. D., Sengupta-Irving, T., & Dieckmann, J. (2010). Developing a mathematical vision: Mathematics as a discursive and embodied practice. In J. N. Moschkovich (Ed.), *Language and mathematics education: Multiple perspectives and directions for research* (pp. 29–71). Charlotte, NC: Information Age.

Gutiérrez, R. (2002). Beyond essentialism: The complexity of language in teaching mathematics to Latina/o students. *American Educational Research Journal, 39*(4), 1047–1088.

Gutstein, E., & Peterson, B. (2005). *Rethinking mathematics: Teaching social justice by the numbers.* Milwaukee, WI: Rethinking Schools.

Hoffert, S. B. (2009). Mathematics: The universal language? *Mathematics Teacher, 103*(2), 130–139.

Lucas, T., Villegas, A. M., & Freedson-Gonzalez, M. (2008). Linguistically responsive teacher education: Preparing classroom teachers to teach English language learners. *Journal of Teacher Education, 59*(4), 361–373.

McDonald, M. A. (2005). The integration of social justice in teacher education. *Journal of Teacher Education, 56*(5), 418–435.

McDonald, M. (2007). The joint enterprise of social justice teacher education. *Teachers College Record, 109*(8), 2047–2081.

Milner, R. H., IV (2010). What does teacher education have to do with teaching? Implications for diversity studies. *Journal of Teacher Education, 61*(1/2), 118–131.

Moschkovich, J. N. (1999). Understanding the needs of Latino students in reform-oriented mathematics classrooms. In W. G. Secada, L. Ortiz-Franco, N. G. Hernandez, & Y. De La Cruz, (Eds.), *Changing the faces of mathematics: Perspectives on Latinos* (pp. 5–12). Reston, VA: National Council of Teachers of Mathematics.

Moschkovich, J. N. (2010a). Language(s) and learning mathematics: Resources, challenges, and issues for research. In J. N. Moschkovich (Ed.), *Language and mathematics education: Multiple perspectives and directions for research* (pp. 1–28). Charlotte, NC: Information Age.

Moschkovich, J. N. (2010b). Recommendations for research on language and mathematics education. In J. N. Moschkovich (Ed.), *Language and mathematics education: Multiple perspectives and directions for research* (pp. 151–170). Charlotte, NC: Information Age.

Murray, O. (2010). A mindfulness to transcend pre-service lip-service: A call for K–12 schools to invest in social justice education. *Multicultural Education, 17*(3), 48–50.

Schleppegrell, M. (2001). Linguistic features of the language of schooling. *Linguistics and Education, 12*(4), 431–459.

Schleppegrell, M. J. (2004). *The language of schooling: A functional linguistic perspective.* Mahwah, NJ: Erlbaum.

Schleppegrell, M. J. (2007). The linguistic challenges of mathematics teaching and learning: A research review. *Reading & Writing Quarterly, 23*(2), 139–159.

Schleppegrell, M. J. (2010). Language in mathematics teaching and learning: A research review. In J. N. Moschkovich (Ed.), *Language and mathematics education: Multiple perspectives and directions for research* (pp. 73–112). Charlotte, NC: Information Age.

Sleeter, C. E. (2009). Teacher education, neoliberalism, and social justice. In W. Ayers, T. Quinn, & D. Stovall (Eds.), *Culturally relevant pedagogy: Clashes and confrontations* (pp. 89–112). New York, NY: Routledge.

Solano-Flores, G. (2006). Language, dialect, and register: Sociolinguistics and the estimation of measurement error in the testing of English language learners. *Teachers College Record, 108*(11), 2354–2379.

Solano-Flores, G. (2010). Function and form in research on language and mathematics education. In J. N. Moschkovich (Ed.), *Language and mathematics education: Multiple perspectives and directions for research* (pp. 113–149). Charlotte, NC: Information Age.

U.S. Census Bureau (2005). *American community survey.* Retrieved from http://factfinder.census.gov/servlet.

Villegas, A. M., & Lucas, T. (2002). Preparing culturally responsive teachers: Rethinking the curriculum. *Journal of Teacher Education, 53*(1), 20–32.

Zeichner, Z. (2009). *Teacher education and the struggle for social justice.* New York, NY: Routledge.

CHAPTER 10

MATHEMATICS + SOCIAL JUSTICE = A NEW TAKE ON MATHEMATICS TEACHER PREPARATION

Caitlyn Holleran and Kadriye El-Atwani

Social justice should be an integral part of mathematics education. There is a widely held belief that the field of mathematics is objective (Herzig, 2005) and does not involve culture, class, or politics (Gutstein, Lipman, Hernandez, & de los Reyes, 1997). This view of mathematics has "contributed to a cultural blindness to the impact of personal, social, cultural, economic, or political factors on the learning of mathematics" (Herzig, 2005, p. 256). The Western version of mathematics taught in U.S. schools (D'Ambrosio, 1997) is replete with cultural and political connotations that convey certain messages. Perhaps this implicit curriculum is a contributing factor to the well-documented disparities in achievement among African American, Latino, Native American, and lower-income students when compared to their White and Asian American counterparts (Martin, 2003).

Despite efforts in the mathematics education community to achieve equity, "the performance gaps among students from various cultural, racial,

Teacher Education for Social Justice: Perspectives and Lessons Learned, pages 115–126.

ethnic, and socioeconomic backgrounds, and those designated with special needs, have persisted" (NCTM Research Committee, 2005, p. 92). Mathematics is thought to be such a powerful subject that other fields of study continually rely upon and employ mathematical concepts (Herzig, 2005). Consequently, the teaching of mathematics is a topic of great importance in education. If beginning teachers know how to teach mathematics for social justice, then perhaps the performance gap will close and students will have equal opportunities to enter the fields of their choice. It is up to mathematics teacher preparation programs to prepare preservice teachers in mathematics for social justice, instilling a sense of moral obligation for equity and demonstrating that social justice in mathematics is possible and necessary.

In this chapter, we outline a social justice-integrated mathematics course for undergraduate students. Teaching preservice teachers how to integrate social justice in their classrooms is a complex issue, given the existence of high-stakes tests, content standards, and the explicit and implicit knowledge that composes mathematics curricula. We have attempted to describe a course that addresses this issue, a course that universities across the country could use to prepare teachers to teach mathematics for social justice.

DEFINING SOCIAL JUSTICE

Before describing our course and its content, it is important to discuss our view of social justice. There is no agreed-upon social justice definition in the current literature, and many in the field of education have their own interpretation of the phrase. For this chapter, our definition of teaching for social justice was influenced by Chubbuck (2010). She defines social justice teaching in three parts: (a) the methods, activities, and expectations teachers have that improve learning opportunities for each individual student; (b) changing educational structures and policies that oppress student learning opportunities; and (c) looking beyond the school and transforming societal structures that perpetuate injustice. We also believe the ultimate goal of teaching for social justice is to create a truly democratic society wherein "all members of that society have equitable opportunities" (Herzig, 2005, p. 254).

Teaching mathematics for social justice would deal with issues of equity within the framework of a mathematics classroom. Gutiérrez (2002) has defined equity in mathematics education as "the inability to predict mathematics achievement and participation based solely on student characteristics such as race, class, ethnicity, sex, beliefs, and proficiency in the dominant language" (p. 153). Therefore, the ultimate goal of teaching mathematics for social justice is to raise the achievement of every student to an equal level and eliminate the correlation between success in mathematics and certain student backgrounds. It is also helpful for teachers to view equity not only as "something to be achieved in mathematics education" but also "envision equity and social justice as something to be attained through mathematics education" (NCTM Research Committee, 2005, p. 98). Teaching mathematics for social justice extends far beyond the mathematics classroom, thus supporting this chapter's initial assertion that social justice must become an indispensable part of mathematics education.

THEORETICAL BACKGROUND

We based the creation of this course on the "Theory of Teacher Preparation" as detailed by Cochran-Smith (2010). In this chapter, we attempt to answer her question, "How can we conceptualize teacher preparation intended to prepare teachers to engage in practice that enhances justice?" (p. 458) as it applies to mathematics education. Of Cochran-Smith's four key issues in teacher preparation, our proposed course falls under the issue of curriculum in teacher education programs. We selected readings and developed assignments that "include opportunities for candidates to learn about subject matter, pedagogy, culture, language, the social and cultural contexts of schooling, and the purposes of education" (p. 459) and allow preservice teachers to unpack these issues before heading into the classroom.

COURSE DESCRIPTION

The purpose of our proposed course, "Learning to Teach Mathematics for Social Justice," is to focus preservice mathematics teachers' attention on issues of social justice, equity, and culturally responsive teaching. This course was created for all preservice mathematics teachers in their third or fourth year of the teacher preparation program. While writing the course objectives, we were influenced by Kumashiro's (2001) belief that the juxtaposition of different ideas, voices, or views does not necessarily lead educators to find real "truth," but it can give them a different approach to thinking, ultimately resulting in either oppressive or anti-oppressive action. With this in mind, we developed the following course objectives: (a) to provide sustainable and practical sources related to social justice in education; (b) to specifically focus on how the theoretical knowledge of social justice can be applied to mathematics education; (c) to analyze all sources of knowledge during field experience observations; (d) to practice applications of preparing classroom materials that support social justice; (e) to evaluate the material of mathematics education with a social justice perspective; and (f) to apply social justice in the classroom.

The course will be divided into three sections. The first part of the semester will cover the definition of social justice and its theoretical base, the second section will focus on literature that incorporates social justice theory into mathematics education, and the third section of the course will give preservice teachers an opportunity to move from theories of mathematics for social justice to practice. We have included a list of suggested readings for the first two sections of the course in the Appendix. These are readings that would be useful in ones' own understanding of mathematics for social justice but can be adjusted based on the needs of the course and the students enrolled. There will be papers and projects due throughout the course, all of which are detailed in the following sections. Finally, this course was developed with an adjoining field experience component in a mathematics classroom that works to achieve equity. It is important for preservice teachers to take their new knowledge of social justice and apply it in a real classroom setting.

Section 1: Social Justice Definitions and Theories

As mentioned earlier, the first aim of this course is to provide a general theoretical background on social justice, focusing on the areas of social justice, multicultural education, and culturally responsive pedagogy (CRP). Moreover, building a sociocultural consciousness for preservice mathematics teachers through reading assignments is a priority. The National Council of Teachers of Mathematics (NCTM, 2005) released a position statement explaining the skills preservice teachers must acquire to be successful mathematics educators. Not only do they need to be mathematically competent and pedagogically proficient, but they also must help to close the achievement gap for students from various backgrounds. In order to meet NCTM's expectations, mathematics teacher educators should increase preservice teachers' knowledge of sociocultural structures in U.S public schools by assigning academic readings that focuses on social justice from various perspectives, including racial, socioeconomic, linguistic, religious, and cultural norms.

The Appendix lists the reading assignments for the first section of this course that aim to develop preservice mathematics teachers' theoretical background knowledge in social justice.

Section 2: Social Justice in Mathematics Education

There have been a few scholars in the field of mathematics education who have written about issues of equity, social justice, and culturally relevant pedagogy as they apply to mathematics (see D'Ambrosio, 1997; Gutiérrez, 2002; Gutstein et al., 1997; Martin, 2000; Stinson, 2006). Since every field differs slightly, it is important for preservice educators to see how these ideas are conceptualized in their specific content area. More importantly, preservice teachers need to discuss how issues of equity, social justice, and CRP affect student identity formation and consequently student performance. Martin (2000) argues that students create their mathematics identity through their beliefs about their "(a) ability to do mathematics, (b) the significance of mathematical knowledge, (c) the opportunities and barriers to enter mathematics fields and (d) the motivation and persistence needed to obtain mathematics knowledge" (p. 19). The readings for this section of the course, as listed in the Appendix, will help preservice teachers discuss these influences on identity formation.

Section 3: Taking Social Justice From Theory to Practice

This last segment of the course will focus less on readings and more on projects and assignments that move preservice teachers from theories of social justice to its praxis. This will be the most challenging part of the course, and consequently, preservice teachers will need support and encouragement from faculty and cooperating teachers. The teacher educator can assign readings from the previous section and ask preservice teachers to link the theories presented in these articles to what they are experiencing in their field classrooms. This section is meant to have a focus on discussion and "brainstorming" so preservice teachers leave the course with an actual conception of mathematics for social justice in their future classroom.

The two projects assigned during Section 3 will require preservice teachers to synthesize their theoretical knowledge and apply it in ways that are similar to what they will be asked to do as full-time teachers. The first major project is a social justice analysis of mathematics textbooks. Ball and Feiman-Nemser (1988)claimed, "The textbook programs that dominate U.S. elementary school classrooms have been criticized for their representation of content; their implicit assumptions about teachers, students, teaching, and learning; and their social and cultural biases" (p. 401). To uncover these implicit assumptions and biases, preservice teachers will study the textbook used in their field placement classroom (if one is used), plus one other book utilized in the school district. The textbooks are to be analyzed for their overall commitment to social justice and equity. The ultimate goal of this assignment is to empower preservice teachers, giving them the tools they will need to shift their future mathematics curriculum to be more socially just. Figure 1 details this project as it would appear in the course syllabus.

The second project in Section 3 involves the careful creation and planning of a socially just mathematics unit to be taught in the field classroom. Downey and Cobbs (2007) assert that, "well-constructed field experiences can help pre-service teachers develop awareness and gain understanding of important cultural considerations related to effective teaching and learning" (p. 391). Preservice teachers need to know and embrace these important cultural considerations if they wish to pursue social justice in their classroom. However, it is important that they have the experience of creat-

Mathematics Textbook Analysis

Main Question: How do mathematics textbooks promote or inhibit mathematics for social justice?

Length of Accompanying Paper: 2 to 3 double-spaced pages.

Description of the assignment: You will look for hidden biases throughout two textbooks: the text used in your field placement classroom and one other math textbook utilized in the school district. Look for the following: ways in which other cultures/ethnicities/differences are portrayed, if at all; contexts of word problems, including the implicit messages sent through the chosen situations; and if the text asks readers to think critically about social structures that perpetuate inequities. Analyze the text and determine *whose knowledge* is portrayed and whose knowledge the text left out. This project will end with a written report that details your findings, and you will suggest possible methods to make the mathematics course more socially just. For this last part, you have the option of suggesting ways for textbooks to incorporate a social justice perspective, or you can suggest supplements to use in contrast to the textbook.

FIGURE 1. Mathematics Textbook Analysis.

ing a unit in its entirety. The unit would describe activities, assessments, and lessons that have a social justice aim, since this is something the preservice teachers will be expected to do in their own classroom. Not only will this assignment help our preservice teachers in the future (Figure 2) when they are in their own classrooms, but it will help them make the connections between theories of social justice and its practice.

Other Assignments and Activities

After the 1980s, teacher narratives were used by teacher education programs to organize data and encourage classroom sharing (Alsup, 2010).

Mathematics for Social Justice Content Unit

Main Question: What does mathematics for social justice look like in the classroom?

Description of the assignment: You will design a unit on a topic of your choosing (discussed in advance with your cooperating teacher) that fully incorporates social justice into mathematics. You will then teach two lessons from this unit in your field classroom. Your unit should be reflective of your particular classroom composition and student needs. This will require a thorough knowledge of the community, student backgrounds, and student beliefs about the value and usefulness of mathematics in their lives. The unit must align with state academic content standards, since this is a requirement all teachers must fulfill. This unit is not a collection of lesson plans, per se, but a collection of activities and pedagogies that have a social justice perspective, yet student learning still occurs. The unit will include ideas for formative and summative assessments, but you must present alternative assessment ideas to replace the usual end-of-unit paper-and-pencil test.

FIGURE 2. Mathematics for Social Justice Content Unit.

Remembering "Social Justice" Through My K–12 Years

Main Question: How have my experiences influenced my beliefs about social justice in education, antibias education, education for equity, and the needs of diverse students?

Length: 3 to 5 double-spaced pages.

Description of the assignment: Writing an autobiography should help you think critically about your own experiences with social justice in education. Try to focus on experiences you encountered in the classroom instead of a detailed account of your schooling. You can provide a brief synopsis of your school environment and community, but you need to specifically focus on any experiences (favorite teacher's instruction, extracurricular activities, field trips, etc.) that illustrate equity, individual needs, cultural differences, and social justice. Most importantly, at the end of your paper, you will provide a separate section addressing *"How does my educational background support the necessity for social justice in education?"*

FIGURE 3.   Remembering Social Justice.

Writing a personal narrative is an important starting point for this course. These narratives will focus on equity, individual differences, and social justice, and will be shared in the classroom. Even though there are potential downfalls to the sharing of these narratives (see Cochran-Smith, 2004), this part of the assignment is critical in order to discuss personal biases and expose the typical White, middle class and monolingual preservice teacher to the experiences of classmates from different backgrounds (Achinstein & Athanases, 2010). Because the beginning of this course focuses on social justice in general, not just in mathematics, the narrative will cover preservice teachers' personal experiences with social justice issues. Figure 3 shows the syllabus assignment for the narrative.

The core of field experience in teacher preparation programs is typically the student teaching experience, a time when the preservice teacher assumes all teaching responsibility under the joint supervision of a cooperating teacher and university supervisor. During the field experience placement, cooperating teachers as well as institutional and classroom-based factors may influence preservice teachers to develop increasingly conservative, traditional, impersonal, and bureaucratic beliefs and practices (Zeichner, 1980). A field experience component is necessary to give preservice students a chance to practice what they have learned about social justice in education through field placement. Figure 4 presents detailed information about the journal assignments of this course that would accompany the field experience observations.

In order to have future teachers ready to teach for social justice, CRP, and multicultural education, teacher educators should provide sustainable

Reflection on "Social Justice" From Field Experience

Main Question: How does my supervising teacher describe, explain, and address issues of diversity and equity in the classroom?

Length: 2 to 3 double-spaced pages

Description of the entries: It is important that you experience the life and responsibilities of a teacher in order to assist you with your decision to become a professional educator. It is even more important that this field experience focuses on teaching mathematics for social justice. By the end of the course, you will write five journals that synthesize all of your observation experiences. Therefore, be cognizant of each journal topic going into the field; this will help you remember specifics when it comes time to write your journals. Below are possible journal themes.

1. Why and how does my supervisor teacher apply NCTM's equity principles in her/ his classroom?
2. Why and how does my supervisor teacher teach mathematics to diverse learners (e.g., English language learners, students of different cultures, "gifted" students, students with disabilities)? What type of interactions have I observed between the teacher and learners?
3. What did you learn from the field experience that will help you be a more effective, socially just teacher?
4. What suggestions would you give to make your specific classroom and/or school more socially just?
5. How have your views of teaching mathematics for social justice and teaching mathematics to diverse learners changed over the course of your field experience?

FIGURE 4. Reflections from field experience.

sources of information for their preservice teachers. As mentioned in Cochran-Smith (2010), teacher education for social justice is not only about methods and practices, but also the intellectual development of preservice teachers. Therefore, teacher educators need to lay the groundwork of social justice theory in their courses. Moreover, teacher educators should consciously develop the theoretical knowledge of preservice teachers. In order to do this, educators could assign reflection papers over the course readings. Figure 5 represents the reflection papers assignments for this course.

Zeichner (2009) discusses social justice in teacher education in terms of different perspectives such as professional development, social reconstruction, teacher organization, and reflections of a university-based teacher education. Additionally, he mentions how the understanding of field experience should be structured with the help of experienced faculty members. To continue moving teacher education away from the traditional sink-or-swim model of field experience, teacher education programs should resemble professional development or partner schools in which university faculty and staff provide instruction about teaching contexts (Zeichner, 2009).

Reflection on Theoretical Framework of Social Justice

(Reflection Entries)
Main Question: What are the issues this reading raises?
Length: 1 to 2 double-spaced pages.
Description of the papers: Writing reflection papers is a simple way to demonstrate that you have thought about the assigned reading critically and are well prepared for class discussions. In the reflection papers, discuss what you have learned about teaching for social justice and how it will assist you in teaching mathematics or in furthering your academic goals. The paper may argue an issue raised by the author, comment on relevant points that the author left out of the reading, and/or include questions that arose while reading. The following are general questions that your reflection paper should cover. • What questions does the writer set out to answer? • How does the author answer his/her question? • How would you evaluate the evidence the author uses to support his/her position? • Do you agree with the points the author makes in the reading? Why or why not? • What issues need further exploration?

FIGURE 5.   Reflections on theory.

The collaboration of public school teachers, university faculty, and preservice teachers not only exemplifies social justice but it also helps preservice teachers feel a sense of power in their field placement. New teachers tend to follow dominant values because they feel powerless to make change (Achinstein & Athanases, 2010). To combat this feeling of powerlessness, we propose an end-of-course classroom gathering for all mentor teachers,

How Can We Have Social Justice-Integrated Mathematics Classrooms in Our Community? The Perspectives of Teachers, Academics, and Prospective Teachers

Main Question: How can we integrate social justice in mathematics classrooms in our community?
Description of Assignment: At the end of semester, we will have a conference with mentor teachers. For this assignment, you should inform your mentor teacher at the beginning of your field experience about this event in order to let them organize their calendar accordingly. The course instructor will also contact each mentor teacher and invite them personally. You will be responsible for leading the conference discussions. You can do this individually or with a group. In class, we will discuss some potential questions that can be used during the conference. During the semester, the course instructor will ask that you specify your role for the conference and according to this, we will build a conference agenda.

FIGURE 6.   Education community discussion.

preservice teachers in the course, and the course instructor. This meeting will address the issues of university-school collaboration in social justice mathematics education. The attendees will spend the evening discussing social justice in math education, sharing teaching experiences, and reflecting upon their role in preparing future educators to teach for social justice. The preservice teachers will be expected to lead the discussions, but the conference can be a fairly structured discussion or more of an open forum. The complete assignment is detailed in Figure 6.

These suggested assignments are meant to develop and solidify a preservice mathematics teacher's ideas of social justice, what forms social justice can take in the mathematics classroom, and the importance of equity and culturally responsive teaching. After experiencing the three sections of the course and completing the field experience and assignments detailed earlier, a preservice teacher will be prepared to teach in a diverse setting, employing the philosophy of social justice and equity in mathematics.

CONCLUSION

The proposed course, "Learning to Teach Mathematics for Social Justice," is conveniently split into three sections to maximize preservice teachers' understanding of social justice in the mathematics classroom. The class will spend time studying and discussing the theoretical underpinnings of social justice, then analyze the literature on social justice in mathematics, and conclude the course with discussions and opportunities to put theory into practice. Assignments and activities have been suggested to aid preservice teachers in this transition from theory to practice, which are vital if Colleges of Education want graduates to pursue social justice after completing their program.

A course for preservice teachers that addresses mathematics for social justice is needed in every teacher preparation program. These programs need to prepare their teachers to work in a diverse world and educate children in a manner that ensures equitable learning (and, by implication, life) opportunities. This chapter illustrates such a course and shows that social justice and mathematics education are not mutually exclusive. If teachers are a part of a teacher preparation program that is infused with the ideals of social justice, then schools can become more equitable institutions for all children.

APPENDIX: SUGGESTED COURSE READINGS

Section 1

Agarwal, R., Epstein, S., Oppenheim, R., Oyler, C., & Sonu, D. (2010). From ideal to practice and back again: Beginning teachers teaching for social justice. *Journal of Teacher Education, 61*(3), 237–247.

de Oliveira, L. C., & Athanases, S. Z. (2007). Graduates' reports of advocating for English language learners. *Journal of Teacher Education, 58*(3), 202–215.

Downey, J. A., & Cobbs, G. A. (2007). "I actually learned a lot from this": A field assignment to prepare future pre-service math teachers for culturally diverse classrooms. *School Science and Mathematics, 107*(1), 391–403.

Gay, G. (2002). Preparing for culturally responsive teaching. *Journal of Teacher Education, 53*(2), 106–116.

Johnson, T. S. (2010). Practice what you preach: A personal and pedagogical social justice policy. In sj Miller & D. Kirkland (Eds.), *Change matters: Critical essays on moving social justice research from theory to policy* (pp. 33–40). New York, NY: Peter Lang.

North, C. E. (2008). What is all this talk about "social justice"? Mapping the terrain of education's latest catchphrase. *Teachers College Record, 110*(6), 1182–1206.

Shoffner, M., & Brown, M. (2010). From understanding to application: The difficulty of culturally responsive teaching as a beginning English teacher. In L. Scherff & K. Spector (Eds.), *Culturally relevant pedagogy: Clashes and confrontations* (pp. 89–112). Lanham, MD: Rowman & Littlefield.

Section 2

Averill, R., Anderson, D., Easton, H., Te Maro, P., Smith, D., & Hynds, A. (2009). Culturally responsive teaching of mathematics: Three models from linked studies. *Journal for Research in Mathematics Education, 40*(2), 157–186.

Brown, R. (2009). Teaching for social justice: Exploring the development of student agency through participation in the literacy practices of a mathematics classroom. *Journal of Mathematics Teacher Education, 12,* 171–185.

Ensign, J. (2003). Including culturally relevant math in an urban school. *Educational Studies, 34*(4), 414–423.

Gutstein, E. (2003). Teaching and learning mathematics for social justice in an urban, Latino school. *Journal for Research in Mathematics Education, 34*(1), 37–73.

Gutstein, E., & Peterson, B. (2005). *Rethinking mathematics: Teaching social justice by the numbers.* Milwaukee, WI: Rethinking Schools.

Gutstein, E., Lipman, P., Hernandez, P. I., & de los Reyes, R. (1997). Culturally relevant mathematics teaching in a Mexican American context. *Journal for Research in Mathematics Education, 28*(6), 709–737.

Leonard, J., Brooks, W., Barnes-Johnson, J., & Berry, R. Q. (2010). The nuances and complexities of teaching mathematics for cultural relevance and social justice. *Journal of Teacher Education, 61*(3), 261–270.

Martin, D. B. (2003). Hidden assumptions and unaddressed questions in *Mathematics for All* rhetoric. *The Mathematics Educator, 13*(2), 7–21.

REFERENCES

Achinstein, B., & Athanases, S. Z. (2010). New teacher induction and mentoring for educational change. In A. Hargreaves, M. Fullan, D. Hopkins, & A. Lieberman (Eds.), *Second international handbook of educational change* (pp. 573–593). New York, NY: Springer.

Alsup, J. (2010). Beyond member checks: Moving toward transformative data analysis. In sj Miller & D. Kirkland (Eds.), *Change matters: Critical essays on moving social justice research from theory to policy* (pp. 97–104). New York, NY: Peter Lang.

Ball, D. L., & Feiman-Nemser, S. (1988). Using textbooks and teachers' guides: A dilemma for beginning teachers and teacher educators. *Curriculum Inquiry, 18*(4), 401–423.

Chubbuck, S. M. (2010). Individual and structural orientations in socially just teaching: Conceptualization, implementation, and collaborative work. *Journal of Teacher Education, 61*(3), 197–210.

Cochran-Smith, M. (2004). *Walking the road: Race, diversity, and social justice in teacher education.* New York, NY: Teachers College Press.

Cochran-Smith, M. (2010). Toward a theory of teacher education for social justice. In A. Hargreaves, M. Fullan, D. Hopkins, & A. Lieberman (Eds.), *Second international handbook of educational change* (pp. 445–467). New York, NY: Springer.

D'Ambrosio, U. (1997). Diversity, equity, and peace: From dream to reality. In J. Trentacosta & M. J. Kenney (Eds.), *Multicultural and gender equality in the mathematics classroom: The gift of diversity* (pp. 243–248). Reston, VA: National Council of Teachers of Mathematics.

Downey, J. A., & Cobbs, G. A., (2007). "I actually learned a lot from this": A field assignment to prepare future pre-service math teachers for culturally diverse classrooms. *Journal of School Science and Math, 107*(1), 391–403.

Gutiérrez, R. (2002). Enabling the practice of mathematics teachers in context: Towards a new equity research agenda. *Mathematical Thinking and Learning, 4*(2/3), 145–187.

Gutstein, E., Lipman, P., Hernandez, P. I., & de los Reyes, R. (1997). Culturally relevant mathematics teaching in a Mexican American context. *Journal for Research in Mathematics Education, 28*(6), 709–737.

Herzig, A. H. (2005). Goals for achieving diversity in mathematics classrooms. *Mathematics Teacher, 99*(4), 253–259.

Kumashiro, K. K. (2001) "Posts'" perspectives on anti-oppressive education in social studies, English, mathematics, and science classrooms. *Educational Researcher, 30*(3), 3–12.

Martin, D. B. (2000). *Mathematics success and failure among African American youth: The roles of sociohistorical context, community forces, school influence, and individual agency.* Mahwah, NJ: Lawrence Erlbaum.

Martin, D. B. (2003). Hidden assumptions and unaddressed questions in *Mathematics for All* rhetoric. *The Mathematics Educator, 13*(2), 7–21.

National Council of Teachers of Mathematics. (2005). *Closing the achievement gap.* Retrieved from http://www.nctm.org/uploadedFiles/About_NCTM/Position_Statements/achievement_gap.pdf

NCTM Research Committee. (2005). Equity in school mathematics education: How can research contribute. *Journal for Research in Mathematics Education, 36*(2), 92–100.

Stinson, D. (2006). African American male adolescents, schooling (and mathematics): Deficiency, rejection, and achievement. *Review of Educational Research, 76*(4), 477–506.

Zeichner, K. M. (1980). Myths and realities: Field-based experiences in pre-service teacher education. *Journal of Teacher Education, 31*(6), 45–49, 51–55.

Zeichner, K. (2009). *Teacher education and the struggle for social justice.* New York, NY: Routledge.

CHAPTER 11

THE UNINTENDED CONSEQUENCES OF NO CHILD LEFT BEHIND ON AN INDIANA SCHOOL CORPORATION

Implications for English Language Learners' Advocates

April M. Burke

Cochran-Smith et al. (2009) state, "Teacher education for social justice is an agenda that not only does not shortchange attention to students' learning but in fact makes enhancing students' learning and their life chances its core commitment" (p. 349). Further, they contend that teaching for social justice "reflects a central and essential purpose of teaching in a democratic society, wherein the teacher is an advocate for students whose work supports larger efforts for social change" (p. 349). In order for future teachers to become self-advocates and advocates for their colleagues and students, they need to understand the power relations that exist between teachers, administrators, policymakers, and other educational stakeholders. Current-

Teacher Education for Social Justice: Perspectives and Lessons Learned, pages 127–140.
Copyright © 2013 by Information Age Publishing
127

ly, these power relations are largely influenced by the No Child Left Behind Act of 2001 (NCLB).

Under NCLB, states are required to assess all school-aged students annually with standardized exams. Test results are used to determine whether or not a school has made adequate yearly progress (AYP). For example, a school can be deemed "in need of improvement" because one of its subgroups did not make AYP. Students are categorized into subgroups if they identify as an ethnic minority, English language learners (ELLs), have a disability, or if they receive free or reduced-price lunch. Schools that do not make AYP enter improvement status and are required to take a number of corrective actions. Lack of school funding to improve programming, use of test results to rank and compare schools, and the impact of annual testing on students and teachers has caused NCLB to become a very controversial law.

Indiana has the third-fastest growing ELL population in the nation. The rate of ELL enrollment in Indiana increased 407.8% (from 6,293 to 31,956 students) from the 1994–1995 to the 2004–2005 school years (U.S. Department of Education, 2006). As in other states, ELLs in Indiana consistently receive lower scores than non-ELLs on the state standardized exam, the Indiana Statewide Testing for Educational Progress Plus (ISTEP+). For example, only 52% of ELLs in grades 3–11 passed the Language/Arts section of the 2007 ISTEP+ compared with 78% of the non-ELLs who passed the exam (Indiana Department of Education, 2009). It should be noted that while the authors of the ISTEP+ use the term Limited English Proficient (LEP) to refer to students who are learning English as a second or additional language, this chapter uses the term English language learner (ELL) to avoid the negative connotation of the word "limited."

Despite Indiana's growing ELL population and the use of the ISTEP+ to assess school performance, few studies examine the use of the ISTEP+ with ELLs. This chapter provides the results of a study that addresses this deficit. The study's primary research question was, What impact has NCLB and the ISTEP+ had on a school corporation with a large ELL population? This overarching question was supplemented with several secondary research questions, including, Do teachers and administrators find the ISTEP+ results to be useful? What are administrators' and teachers' perceptions of factors influencing ELL performance on the ISTEP+?

This chapter begins by explaining the exams and measures used to hold schools accountable in the state of Indiana. This section focuses on accountability measures as they relate to the schooling experience of ELLs. Then the study's methodology and results are explained. The chapter concludes with implications of the results for teacher educators, aspiring teachers, and other advocates who seek to address the unintended consequence of NCLB for schools serving ELLs.

STANDARDIZED TESTS, SCHOOL ACCOUNTABILITY IN INDIANA, AND MATTERS OF SOCIAL JUSTICE

The ISTEP+ is designed to measure student progress on questions related to the *Indiana Academic Standards*. Almost all students in grades three through eight are required to take the ISTEP+. Students with certain disabilities are given alternative assessments, and newcomer ELLs receive a one-time exemption from taking the ISTEP+ (Indiana University, 2007). Thereafter, accommodations may be provided for ELLs who have not been classified as Above Proficiency (Level 5) or Fluent English Proficient (FEP) based on their LAS Links score. The LAS Links is an English language proficiency exam that is used to place English learner students, to measure their progress in attaining English language skills, and to determine when students no longer need language services.

To demonstrate AYP and avoid sanctions, school corporations in Indiana are required to make annual measurable achievement objectives (AMAOs). To make its AMAOs, a school corporation must demonstrate that their ELL students are making progress in three different ways. First, a certain percentage of ELLs must show progress in attaining English. Second, a certain percentage of ELLs must attain English proficiency or become reclassified as FEP. Third, ELLs must make AYP on the ISTEP+. Schools that fail to make AMAOs for 4 or more years are required to undergo restructuring and may face staff layoffs and a reduction in funding (Walker, 2010).

Undoubtedly, NCLB has caused increased attention to be paid to ELLs; however, researchers such as Kate Menken (2008) contend that the attention paid has been largely negative. In her book, *English Learners Left Behind: Standardized Testing as Language Policy*, Menken examines the use of standardized tests with ELLS in New York. She concludes that the proliferation of standardized test use has had far-reaching and negative consequences for ELLs, including increased drop-out rates and teachers teaching to the test.

Prospective ELL educators need to be informed about the realities they will face in the classroom and school environment. Unfortunately, there are often disconnects between the materials covered in teacher education programs and the lived experiences of educators in the field. Reynolds and Brown (2010) summarize Westheimer and Suurtamm's (2008) argument by stating, "Teacher education must focus on how to bridge the gap between what is espoused in theory lessons about social justice and what happens in reality in schools and communities" (p. 411). This chapter elucidates ways in which education professionals respond to the mandates of NCLB; the administrators discuss unexpected challenges they encountered as a result of NCLB and their opinions regarding the benefits and downfalls of school accountability. The intent of this chapter is to provide teacher educators and future teachers, especially those who intend to work with ELLs, a basis for discussing teaching for social justice in the current era of high-stakes testing.

METHODOLOGY

The study took place in a rural Indiana town that was given the pseudonym Greenbush. The study took place in a rural Indiana town that was given the pseudonym Greenbush. According to the 2000 U.S. Census, Greenbush is predominately White. However, Greenbush has a growing Hispanic population, which in 2000 constituted approximately a fifth of the population. Currently, Greenbush School Corporation (GSC) runs three elementary schools, which were given the following pseudonyms: Somerset (grades K–5), Brewer (grades K–2), and Mason (grades 3–5). All three schools receive Title I funding.

The study was primarily qualitative. During the spring of 2009, interviews were conducted with three GSC administrators. Their pseudonyms and job titles are as follows: Chad King, an elementary school principal; Sarah Kroger, the Title I director, and Rosa O'Connel, the ELL coordinator. Transcripts were analyzed using the constant-comparative method, which involves repeated reviewing, coding, and sorting of text into categories (Coffey & Atkinson, 1996; Merriam, 1998).

Quantitative data was included for triangulation purposes, that is, to support or draw into question the conclusions reached through the qualitative analysis. For example, students' ISTEP+ scores were examined to verify the participants' assertions that ELLs at or below Level 3 on the LAS Links would be unlikely to pass the ISTEP+. Student test data came from the Indiana Department of Education's website (www.doe.in/gov) and from the school corporation.

RESULTS

The study's original purpose was to investigate the impact of NCLB and the ISTEP+ on the Greenbush School Corporation; however, due to the study's exploratory nature, the process of data collection and analysis brought a number of other, related issues to light. For example, the administrators' comments raise serious concerns regarding the appropriateness of the accommodations made for ELLs on the ISTEP+ as well as the validity of the exam when used with ELLs who are not FEP.

This section provides a summary of the study's results, which may be of particular interest and use to those concerned with the ways in which NCLB is affecting schools with diverse populations. The study is limited in that it provides only the perspectives of three administrators from one school corporation. That being said, the issues they describe are not trivial, but indicative of the span of concerns facing teachers and administrators not only in the state of Indiana but nationwide. This study highlights why it is difficult for schools with diverse populations and large ELL populations to make AYP and avoid the stigma of being labeled "failing" schools; it also illustrates the tactics used by school personnel and administrators in particular to meet the mandates of NCLB. This section is followed by a discussion section that describes the practical implications of the study's findings for teacher educators, prospective teachers, and other advocates who seek to establish and maintain equitable school environments and assessments for all learners.

Making Adequate Yearly Progress (AYP) by "Playing the Numbers Game"

For Principal Chad King, making AYP is a top concern. Schools that do not make AYP are required to develop school improvement plans. Chad said AYP drives his school's improvement plan and that he is constantly thinking about it. Chad and the Title I director, Sarah Kroger, explained that an important component of Greenbush School Corporation's plan is a program called Response to Intervention (RTI). RTI is used to identify and assist struggling learners. Chad explained that his school has an intervention block that is used to help the "bottom 20%" of students, not including students identified for special education services. During the intervention block, ELLs and low-performing students receive additional help. Students are periodically regrouped according to their performance on different assessments.

To compensate for the challenges ELLs face when taking standardized exams in a language they have not fully mastered, NCLB allows test accommodations to be made for ELLs, and the law includes a safe harbor provision. A school makes safe harbor if the percentage of its ELL population that failed a standardized exam is reduced by 10 percent from the previous year (U.S. Department of Education, 2009). Chad explained that in order for his school to make safe harbor, roughly 10 to 12 more ELL students would need to pass the next ISTEP+.

In the following quote, Sarah Kroger explains how the school corporation is focusing its intervention on the lower-performing students. She matter-of-factly explained that they are now playing a numbers game.

> And now, the one thing that we have done is we have really focused our intervention. We're playing the numbers game. We're looking at where our cutoff was. What the cutoff was for passing or not passing and we've taken the kids that are only like 10 points away from passing and we've focused our intervention on those guys. If we're only passing at 50%, we're not going to the next year pass at 75 percent. We know that. But, if you can increase it 10 percent you will make AYP. You don't have to get all the way to the 70 some percent, you can increase 10 percent. In some cases, at grade level, that's only about 10 kids. It's not like you're talking about we have to get 300 kids to pass

next spring. So, we're starting to play that numbers game now. If we can get those 10 extra kids, plus count on those kids that maybe, just barely passed. We're focusing our intervention on these kids and we're doing it that route. And we're not the only corporation that plays that. That's just what everybody does at this point

While discussing their approach to increasing the number of students who pass the ISTEP+, Chad and Sarah lamented the fact that the ISTEP+ does not follow a growth model. They explained that the population being tested one year may or may not be the same population being tested the following year.

Chad said it was very difficult to use ISTEP+ results to measure the progress of individual students or to use the results to improve classroom instruction. The task of following individuals becomes more complicated if they move between schools. He explained,

> Our transient kids move in and out, everywhere around. That affects your percentages from year to year. So, it's really tough to say, "Well, this group of students is doing well—they're progressing." You can follow those specific kids, but it's a lot of work to figure out who's done what. Like my fifth grade [class], it's almost 200 kids. So, you have to figure out, okay, who's moved in? Who hasn't? Who's been here the whole time?

Sarah echoed Chad's sentiments regarding the difficulty of using ISTEP+ results to monitor student progress or improve classroom instruction. In addition, Chad and Sarah said it was difficult and time-consuming to garner useful information from the current online ISTEP+ data system and convert the results into information that could be used to inform instruction. Both advocated returning to the previous system in which hardcopies of ISTEP+ score reports and actual student exams were disseminated to schools.

Since the completion of this study, Indiana implemented a growth model based on the Colorado growth model developed by Damian Betebenner. Indiana's growth model classifies students as having attained high, typical, or low growth. More information is available at the Indiana Department of Education's Learning Connection website (https://learningconnection. doe.in.gov/).

Emotions Toward and Resistance to Testing

All three administrators, Sarah, Chad, and Rosa O'Connel, the ELL coordinator, mentioned that there was resistance toward high-stakes testing from students and teachers. Chad said that by the end of testing week, the students are listless and apathetic. Some put their heads down, sigh loudly, or groan. Sarah said teachers "spend more time fighting the data and fighting the state, instead of just saying, 'What do we need to do to make this work?'"

Rosa acknowledged that a positive aspect of NCLB has been an increased attention on the needs of ELLs; however, she is a staunch opponent of having a standards-based curriculum, and she opposes the way standardized tests are being used to assess children. She said that having a standards-based curriculum has lessened the amount of creativity that previously existed in schools. She said, "We're dealing with children who learn at different paces and levels and we can't just cookie-cut them as a product." In addition, the administrators used violent analogies such as "tough battle," "vicious cycle," and "double-edged sword" when discussing the ISTEP+.

Factors Influencing ELL Test Performance

The administrators explained that ELL performance on the ISTEP+ was influenced by the students' abilities, their familiarity with the standardized testing procedure, as well the format of the test and its construction. Chad and Rosa explained that the students' background knowledge, their first language (L1) literacy, their parents' level of literacy, and their socioeconomic status (SES) are all factors that influence their performance. Chad mentioned that ELLs often lack certain test-taking skills, like self-monitoring. Sarah explained ELLs' lack of exposure to test taking in general negatively impacts their performance. She also said that both the vocabulary and sentence structures used in the test can be very challenging for ELLs.

All three administrators believe that ELLs at Levels 1 and 2 on the LAS Links will not be able to pass the ISTEP+. They think that it is unlikely but possible for Level 3s to the pass the test and that Level 4s and definitely Level 5s will be able to pass the test. Rosa expressed a great deal of frustration in regard to the expectation to have all students pass the exam. In the following quote she explains her views:

> They're asking us to do [laughs] almost an impossibility. These students don't have the language. You know, like I said, our Level 4s, most of our Level 4s and up, our Level 5s are passing the ISTEP. They have the language skills to pass this test. But when you don't . . . Levels 1 to 3, how can you possibly ask them to pass a test if they're not proficient in the language to start with?

The assertion made by the administrators that ELLs at Levels 1–3 are not able to pass the ISTEP+ was investigated by examining the scores of free and reduced-price-lunch students.

Table 1 shows the number of free and reduced-price-lunch ELL students by LAS Links Levels and non-ELLs in grades 3–8 who passed or did not pass the English/Language Language Arts portion of the 2007 ISTEP+. Table 1 does not include data on special education students. Figure 1 presents the same data from Table 1 as percentages. For example, of the 73 Level 3 ELLs who took the test, 14 (19%) passed compared to 59 (81%) of those who did not pass.

TABLE 1. Number of Greenbush School Corporation Free and Reduced-Price-Lunch ELLs by LAS Links Levels and Non-ELLs in Grades 3–8 Who Passed and Did Not Pass (DNP) the English/Language Arts Portion of the 2007 ISTEP+

	ELL 1	ELL2	ELL 3	ELL 4	ELL 5	Non ELL
Pass	0	1	14	73	54	236
Did Not Pass	8	16	59	54	5	111
Total	8	17	73	127	59	347

Table 1 and Figure 1 support the assertions made by administrators that ELLs at Levels 1–3 will be unlikely to pass the ISTEP+. This becomes more evident when combining ELLs in different LAS Levels. For example, 83 (85%) of the 98 ELLs at Levels 1–3 did not pass the exam compared to 59 (31%) of the 186 ELLs at Levels 4 and 5. Interestingly, this is roughly comparable to the percentage of non-ELLs (111 out of 347 or 32%) who did not pass the exam.

Schools in Greenbush have failed to make AYP not only because of their ELL students' test performance but also because of their special education student performance. Figure 2 compares the number of free and reduced-price-lunch special education ELL and special education non-ELL students

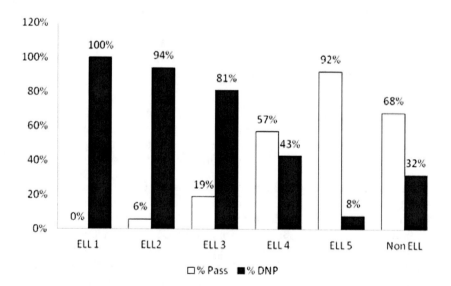

FIGURE 1. Percentage of Greenbush School Corporation free and reduced-price-lunch ELLs by LAS Links levels and non-ELLs in grades 3–8 who passed and did not pass (DNP) the English /Language Arts portion of the 2007 ISTEP+.

☐ Pass ■ Did Not Pass

FIGURE 2. Number of Greenbush School Corporation free and reduced-price-lunch special education ELL and special education non-ELL students in grades 3–8 who passed the English /Language Arts portion of the 2007 ISTEP+.

in grades 3–8 who passed and did not pass the 2007 ISTEP+. Of the 129 ELLs in grades 3–8 who took the exam, only one student categorized as both an ELL and a special education passed the exam. This student was a fourth-grade Level 5 ELL. Of the 97 free and reduced-price-lunch special-education students who took the exam, 89 (92%) did not pass.

This examination of student test performance inspires many questions. Is acquiring English key to ELL success on the ISTEP+? The data indicates that far more ELLs at Levels 4 and 5 pass the exam; however, a large percentage (32%) of non-special-education, non-ELLs also did not pass. Why? Also, what level of English proficiency do ELLs need to attain in order to pass the exam? Lastly, is it fair to assess schools with tests that may not be suited for certain populations, such as ELLs who have a limited grasp of English or students with certain disabilities?

Problems With Test Accommodations for ELLs

The four test accommodations discussed by the administrators were providing extra time, reading portions of the test aloud, administering the test in small groups, and providing students with bilingual dictionaries. While there were differences of opinion regarding the first three, the administrators strongly agreed that the last, providing students with bilingual Spanish-English dictionaries, was not a helpful accommodation because the majority of students are not literate in Spanish nor are they accustomed to using bilingual dictionaries.

Chad and Sarah mentioned that implementing the accommodations was difficult to do and a strain on the staff. In addition, the administrators said that they and the teachers do not receive training on how to administer the

ISTEP+, access test results and information on the Internet, or interpret ISTEP+ scores. Both Sarah and Chad claimed that the test directions were not clear as to how to read portions of the test aloud to ELL students; they said they experimented with how to make this accommodation. Rosa was very adamant that reading the test aloud to students at Levels 1 and 2 would not be helpful, although she did concede that it may be helpful for students at Levels 3 and above.

Alternative Assessment Suggestions

Chad mentioned that formerly an alternative assessment called the Indiana Standards Tool for Alternate Reporting (ISTAR) was available for ELLs with low English language proficiency levels. Information on the ISTAR can be found at the Indiana Department of Educations's website (https://ican. doe.state.in.us/beta/istarinfo.htm). In Chad's school, the ISTAR is used only with special education students. Rosa said that alternative assessments such as portfolios should be used with ELLs at Levels 1–3. Sarah suggested developing a test that assessed the same content but at different language proficiency levels. However, she quickly provided a rebuttal to her own suggestion, stating that the development of such tests would be too expensive and complicated. She added, "And I think it would kind of defeat the purpose of what they're trying to do which is say everybody should be the same and everybody should be held accountable to the same standards."

DISCUSSION

The three administrators who participated in this study were experienced classroom teachers. Thomas (2005) states that much of the collateral damage caused by high-stakes assessments could have been avoided if the views of experienced teachers had been included in the restructuring of school programming (p. 239). He explains that it is teachers who understand better than anyone "the relationship between classroom practice and students' performance on high-stakes tests" (p. 239). This section discusses the information the administrators provided, poses questions, offers possible solutions to some of the problems they raised, and discusses the implications of the study for teacher educators, aspiring teachers, and others who seek to establish and maintain equitable and just schools, assessments, and educational policies.

A primary concern for Greenbush administrators is whether their schools make AYP. The three administrators agree that schools should be held accountable; however, they do not feel that the negative image that their corporation has incurred is warranted. In order to make AYP, Indiana schools with large numbers of students in subgroups must demonstrate that more of those students are passing the ISTEP+. Greenbush schools are diverse; therefore, each year, more of their Hispanic, ELL, special education, and low-SES students must pass the exam.

Because the elementary schools in Greenbush have not made AYP, they have been required to develop improvements plans. Part of their plan includes the implementation of a program called Response to Intervention (RTI). The results of this program will not be evident for several years. Will improvement plans be enough to raise student test performance and save Greenbush schools from ultimately being shut down if they continue to fail to make AYP?

Another pressing question: Is the ISTEP+ appropriate for all students? This study provides evidence that suggests the ISTEP+ may not be a fair or valid measure when used with ELLs at LAS Links Levels 1–3. The fact that 83 of the 98 (85%) of the free and reduced-price-lunch ELLs at Levels 1–3 did not pass the 2007 ISTEP+ is reason for concern. There is also reason to question the appropriateness of this exam for use with special education students since 89 of the 97 (92%) of the free and reduced-price-lunch special education students did not pass.

This study has also raised questions regarding the appropriateness of the test accommodations made for ELLs on the ISTEP+. According to the Indiana Department of Education (2008), "The purpose of testing accommodations is to 'level the playing field,' or to achieve parity with non-disabled, non-language deficient peers in the test-taking situation" (p. 69). According to Young et al. (2008), "At present, because research findings are mixed and inconclusive, no definitive conclusions can be drawn about the effectiveness of different accommodations for ELLs" (p. 172). The fact that the Indiana Department of Education is currently in the process of determining whether or not accommodations negatively or positively impact test scores, thereby affecting the validity of the exam (2008, p. 69), supports Young et al.'s assertion.

The administrators provided valuable information for teacher educators and aspiring teachers. Most importantly, they described how the mandates of NCLB have impacted their work and their corporations. A stated goal of the law is to aid all children in meeting state standards; however, many children are far from achieving that objective. Greenbush administrators crunch numbers and target their resources at students who are on the cusp of passing. They witness frustrated and test-weary teachers and students. Future educators need to be aware of how NCLB will affect their schools, their students, and them personally. School accountability is now expanding into teacher accountability as states implement new methods of assessing teachers based on their students' standardized test performance.

The administrators also described the importance given to standardized test results. Teacher educators need to prepare their students for this reality. In addition to helping future teachers understand how to prepare lessons and work with diverse populations, teacher educators need to discuss the precedence given to test scores as well as state and federal laws. In addition to classroom observations, students in teacher education programs need to conduct research on NCLB and engage in meaningful dialogues with experienced classroom teachers and administrators regarding NCLB policies.

Aspiring teachers need to understand that policies and laws are malleable and that they, in addition to researchers and policymakers, can have an impact on the educational experiences of our nation's children. If they find they are sacrificing meaningful and engaging lessons for test preparation, find test accommodations to be inappropriate, or find a test to be inappropriate for certain learners, it is critical that they become advocates for their students.

Athanases and de Oliveira (2007) investigated the difficulties encountered by new teachers who attempted to act as advocates. Citing the work of Richert (1997), they explain,

> Developing a stance of *advocate* for equity involves several key dimensions. It includes viewing all aspects of school as problematic rather than given; learning to locate expertise inside oneself; and being able to envision how schools can more effectively meet all students' needs. (p. 124, original emphasis)

Athanases and de Oliveira's (2007) research illustrates that serving as an advocate requires persistence and includes a variety of risks (p. 133). Teacher education programs can best prepare new teachers for the challenges they will encounter by providing them with accurate information regarding the political climate of today's schools as well as strategies for promoting equity and fighting for social justice despite their position. Athanases and Martin's (2006) work provides the perspectives of preservice teachers regarding their preparation to become advocates for equity. The teachers indicated a number of factors that contributed to their success, including "explicit teaching of equity issues and pedagogy" and "development of rationales to support equity-oriented instructional approaches" (p. 641).

For new teachers, improving student test scores while simultaneously fighting for greater equity in educational institutions is a daunting task. However, according to research by Bender-Slack and Raupach (2008),there is hope. In their investigation of social studies teachers' perspectives, they concluded that standards-based curricula and teaching for social justice are compatible as long as teachers adopt "the perspective that social justice is an approach rather than a topic" (p. 258). Bender-Slack and Raupach suggest that rather than perceiving themselves confined by a set of rigid standards, teachers should adopt an approach to teaching wherein every lesson provides the opportunity to delve into issues related to social justice.

Hopefully, in addition to experiencing an adequate teacher preparation program, those entering the teaching profession will find inspiration from motivated individuals like Chad, who explained that previously he taught at a small homogeneous school where 80 percent of the students passed the ISTEP+. Working at Greenbush has presented more challenges, but he is both determined and optimistic about improving his school. He explained that he enjoys the challenges: "That's why I like doing what I do. Taking problems and looking at it and figuring out solutions and working at making ourselves better."

CONCLUSION

This study examined the impact of NCLB and a high-stakes test, the ISTEP+, on a school corporation in rural Indiana that has a large English language learner population. The information provided by three administrators in the corporation revealed that the ISTEP+ has had a tremendous impact on their corporation. For example, the school corporation examined, Greenbush School Corporation, implemented a program called Response to Intervention (RTI) to improve students' ISTEP+ scores and meet the demands of NCLB. In addition, the corporation has received a considerable amount of negative publicity because its schools consistently fail to make AYP. Future teachers need to understand the many ways in which NCLB affects public schools and students. In addition, they need to understand that their role is not limited to instruction; they must assume the position of advocates. They are the ones who will witness and experience firsthand the positive and negative consequences of ever-changing education policies. Participating in an effective teacher educational program that is dedicated to promoting teachers as agents of change is key to their success. As future teachers, they should be inspired by the wonders and satisfaction that teaching will bring, but it is critical that they also be prepared to challenge the many injustices they will encounter when working with disadvantaged and minority language students.

REFERENCES

Athanases, S. Z., & de Oliveira, L. C. (2007). Conviction, confrontation, and risk in new teachers' advocating for equity. *Teaching Education, 18*(2), 123–136.

Athanases, S. Z., & Martin, K. J. (2006). Learning to advocate for educational equity in a teacher credential program. *Teaching and Teacher Education, 22*, 627–646.

Bender-Slack, D. & Raupach, M.P. (2008). Negotiating standards and social justice in the social studies: Educators' perspectives. *Social Studies, 99*(6), 255–259.

Cochran-Smith, M., Shakman, K., Jong, C., Terrell, D. G., Barnatt, J., & McQuillan, P. (2009). Good and just teaching: The case for social justice in teacher education. *American Journal of Education, 115*, 347–377.

Coffey, A., & Atkinson, P. (1996). *Making sense of qualitative data analysis: Complementary strategies.* Thousand Oaks, CA: Sage.

Indiana Department of Education. (2008). *2008-2009 ISTEP+ program manual: Policies and procedures for Indiana's assessment system.*

Indiana Department of Education. (2009). *Indiana Department of Education.* Retrieved from http://www.doe.in.gov

Indiana University. (2007, August 7). *Resources, understanding, and inclusiveness are needed for Latino Students in Indiana.* Retrieved from http://site.educ.indiana.edu/ResourcesneededforLatinostudentsinIndiana/tabid/6574/Default.aspx

Menken, K. (2008). *English learners left behind: Standardized testing as language policy.* Clevedon, UK: Multilingual Matters.

Merriam, S. B. (1998). *Qualitative research and case study applications in education.* San Francisco, CA: Jossey Bass.

Reynolds, R., & Brown, J. (2010). Social justice and school linkages in teacher education programmes. *European Journal of Teacher Education, 33*(4), 405–419.

Thomas, R. M. (2005). *High stakes testing: Coping with collateral damage.* Mahwah, NJ: Lawrence Erlbaum.

U.S. Department of Education. (2009). *Indiana Department of Education consolidated state application accountability Workbook.* Retrieved from http://www.ed.gov/admins/lead/account/stateplans03/incsa.pdf

U.S. Department of Education: Office of English Language Acquisition, Language Enhancement, and Academic Achievement for Limited English Proficient Students. (2006). Indiana Rate of LEP Growth 1994/1995-2004/2005. Retrieved from: http://www.ncela.gwu.edu/policy/states/reports/statedata/2004LEP/Indiana-G-05.pdf

Walker, M. (2010). Title III Annual Measurable Achievement Objectives (AMAO) Performance Targets. (Memorandum). Retrieved from http://www.doe.in.gov/super/2010/03-March/031910/documents/memo_title_3.pdf

Westheimer, J., & Suurtamm, K. (2008). The politics of social justice meets practice. Teacher education and school change. In W. Ayers, T. Quinn, & D. Stovall (Eds.), *Handbook of social justice in education* (pp. 589–93). New York, NY: Routledge.

Young, J. W., Cho, Y., Ling, G., Cline, F., Steinberg, J., & Stone, E. (2008). Validity and fairness of state standards-based assessments for English language learners. *Educational Assessment, 13*(2), 170–192.

CONTRIBUTORS

Reiko Akiyama is a doctoral student in curriculum studies at Purdue University and is currently teaching educational courses as a teaching assistant in the College of Education. She completed a Master of Arts in Teaching International Languages (TESOL and Japanese) at California State University, Chico. She has worked as a Japanese instructor at Butte College, Oroville, California, and at a language institute in Taichung, Taiwan. Her areas of research interest are social justice in education and multicultural education. Her dissertation topic focuses on the experience of learning in culturally and linguistically diverse educational environments for adolescent Japanese sojourner students in Indiana.

Maricela Alvarado is a PhD student in Literacy and Language Education in the Department of Curriculum and Instruction at Purdue University. As the director of the Latino Cultural Center at Purdue, she has had the opportunity to build the center's services, programs, and outreach from scratch as she is the inaugural director. Maricela has an MEd from the University of Florida. She is the daughter of Mexican migrants who settled in Washington State, where Maricela was born and raised. Being the first to go to

Teacher Education for Social Justice: Perspectives and Lessons Learned, pages 141–146.
Copyright © 2013 by Information Age Publishing
141

college, Maricela took the detoured route through working and attending community college. Finally, at the age of 27, she graduated from Washington State University.

Ryan Angus is a doctoral candidate in the Literacy and Language Education program at Purdue University. Prior to beginning his graduate work, Ryan completed an MA in English literature at Marshall University and worked as a full-time college writing instructor. He also has several years of experience as a K–12 substitute teacher. Mr. Angus' research interests include Appalachian studies, systemic functional linguistics, social semiotics, writing pedagogies, and language in the content areas.

Zaira R. Arvelo Alicea is a doctoral student in curriculum and instruction at Purdue University, majoring in English education and pursuing a certificate in English language learning. She has a Master of Arts and a bachelor's degree in English education from two different campuses of the University of Puerto Rico. In addition, she has taught for 6 years and has worked as editorial assistant for Purdue University's journal, *First Opinions-Second Reactions*. She coordinates community engagement events with Latino/a families. She is currently a research assistant for Purdue University's Discovery Learning Research Center and a member of the Assessment Committee for the project Instruction Matters: Purdue Academic Course Transformation. Her research focuses on reading as it pertains to Latino/a communities and English language learners. Her dissertation interests include how the paradigms of social imagination and the inclusion of authentic Latino/a aesthetics may aid the literacy development of English language learners.

Thu Ya Aung earned his MSEd in curriculum studies from Purdue University after he had obtained an MA and BA (Honors) degrees in English from University of Yangon, Myanmar. He worked as an instructor in a number of language schools in Myanmar and is now working as a freelance trainer for Access English, The British Council (Burma), and Pyo Pin, a British organization that supports monastic and community schools in Myanmar. His research interests include education for social justice, education of language and cultural minorities, multicultural education, and bilingual education.

April Burke is a PhD candidate in the Literacy and Language Education program at Purdue University. Previously, she was a middle and high school teacher in the state of Maine, where she worked primarily with disadvantaged youth and English learners (ELs). April's research interests include the testing and assessment of ELs, educational policy related to EL and disadvantaged learners, and the impact of the No Child Left Behind Act on public education in the United States. April's dissertation research investigates the performance of ELs from a rural Indiana school corporation on a state standardized test. April's article, co-authored with Luciana C. de Oliveira, titled "Educational Policies in the United States and Implications for English Learners," was published in the *Brazilian Journal of Applied Linguistics* (Revista Brasileira de Linguistica Aplicada) in 2012.

Amy Carey graduated with a Bachelor's of Science from Michigan State University in 2008. She studied Family Community Services with emphases in Early Childhood Education and Diversity. Amy graduated with a Master's of Science from Purdue University in 2011. She studied child development with a special interest in pre-literacy skills and classroom interventions. Her master's thesis focused on teacher's interactions with print and its relation to children's print knowledge in a Head Start sample. Amy currently works as a faculty member at Lansing Community College in Lansing, Michigan. There, she teaches a foundations course in early childhood education for dual-enrolled high school students in partnership with the Eaton County Career Preparation Center. She enjoys being a part of the identity and career formation process for students wishing to pursue careers in education.

Adrien Chauvet is a PhD candidate in the department of Physics at Purdue University, where he is also an instructor in the Physics department. His interest in teaching brings him to regularly take classes in the College of Education and to teach physics at the Islamic School of Indianapolis. He obtained his Bachelor of Science at the Louis-Pasteur University, France, and his master's degree in physics from Purdue University. Adrien's doctoral research is on energy and electron mechanisms in photosynthetic organisms. Certified by the Center of Instructional Excellence at Purdue University, he was also the 2012 recipient of the Akley-Mandler Award for Teaching Excellence from Purdue University as well as the 2012 Outstanding Teaching Assistant from the American Association of Physics Teachers. Through his projects, Adrien aims to give minority students vision to imagine futures in science and engineering.

Shaivi Divatia completed her MSEd at Purdue University in 2012. Shaivi also taught the undergraduate course Teaching English as a New Language (EDCI 370) at Purdue to seniors for two semesters. All these experiences have strengthened her determination to explore avenues that help address the learning difficulties faced by immigrant children while attempting to settle in a new land. Shaivi was born and raised in India and is fluent in three languages: Gujarati, Hindi, and English. Shaivi obtained her undergraduate degree from Gujarat University, Ahmedabad, India, majoring in business and finance. Shaivi also pursued a diploma in creative writing in English from IGNOU, Ahmedabad.

Kadriye El-Atwani is currently a teaching assistant and PhD student in the Department of Curriculum and Instruction at Purdue University. She is broadly interested in teacher education, multicultural education, and social justice. Her dissertation research examines the multicultural education in the context of Islamic schools in the United States. More specifically, she is interested in how Islamic schoolteachers experience multicultural education as internal diversity of Muslim culture is considered. Kadriye received a BS in elementary mathematics education, with an elementary science education minor, from Middle East Technical University, Turkey, in 2005. After working as a mathematics teacher in private and public schools, she decided to enroll for a master's degree in curriculum studies at Purdue, which she completed in 2011.

Mark Haugen is a PhD student in second language studies/English as a second language in the Department of English at Purdue University. He received his MA in educational studies in 2012. His research interests include second language studies, immigrant rights and issues, and critical pedagogy. Mark is originally from Minnesota but has lived in various places, including South Korea and Chile.

Caitlyn Holleran received a master's degree in curriculum and instruction at Purdue University in 2012. While at Purdue, she was interested in a wide variety of topics, such as mathematics equity and the mathematical training of preservice elementary teachers. Originally from Ohio, she studied math education for secondary students at Ohio University and worked as a high school and middle school teacher before going to Purdue as a full-time student. In summer 2012, she has returned to teaching mathematics at the high school level.

Joshua Iddings is a PhD candidate at Purdue University and was born and raised in a small town in the foothills of the Appalachian Mountains in eastern Kentucky. He received his bachelor's degree in English literature from Marshall University in Huntington, West Virginia. After earning his BA, he went on to study English literature, writing pedagogy and systemic functional linguistics at Marshall. His research interests include first and second language writing pedagogy, systemic functional linguistics, teaching for social justice, and Appalachian studies. Currently, Josh is researching the writing practices and pedagogy of 12th-grade students and teachers, respectively, at one Appalachian high school in eastern Kentucky.

Galina Miller completed an MSEd in curriculum studies at Purdue University in 2012. She was born in Russia in a multicultural family and graduated with an MA in linguistics in Russia. She worked for several years as a teacher of English and French languages in a technical college. This teaching experience gave her in-depth insights into the teaching profession, wherein she realized that an educator is a responsible agent in inspiring children for success. For her master's degree, her focus of interest was multicultural education, with a particular interest in the identity negotiation process and its impact on second language acquisition. Galina graduated with honors from Purdue University and continues her research in the field.

David Norris is a continuing lecturer in the Department of Mathematics at Purdue University, teaching undergraduate classes in mathematics. He has a Bachelor of Science in secondary education from West Virginia University and a Master of Science in applied mathematics through Purdue University. He is currently working toward a PhD in mathematics education at Purdue. David spent many years in southside Virginia teaching high school courses in mathematics, chemistry, and physics. For the past several years, he has been teaching undergraduate calculus courses at Purdue. He is currently working in projects on language and discourse in mathematics, writing in the content area, and teacher reflective practices.

Jubin Rahatzad is a PhD student in curriculum studies at Purdue University. He received an MA in political science from Purdue University in 2007. His research interests include critical theories, with emphases on colonial (postcolonial) studies, ecojustice issues, and revitalizing materialist analysis within various areas of critical thought. Professional activities include teaching a foundational multiculturalism and education course, program assistant for a teacher education study-abroad program in Honduras, and research on preservice teachers' cross-cultural experiences and perceptions within study-abroad programs.

Ileana Cortés Santiago is a doctoral student in Literacy and Language Education (English Education) in the Department of Curriculum and Instruction at Purdue University and a graduate assistant with the Butler Center for Leadership Excellence. Her academic formation includes a Master of Arts in English from the University of Puerto Rico (UPR)-Rio Piedras and a bachelor's degree in English from the UPR-Mayaguez. She is currently an AACTE Holmes Diversity Scholar, whose research interests include Latino/a family engagement with an emphasis on literacy, English language learning, and the use of music as a doorway to language development. She has been the recipient of various scholarships and grants for academic achievement and to develop research and engagement projects, both at the college and national level.

Amina Shareef is a master's student in curriculum studies in the Department of Curriculum and Instruction at Purdue University, where she is also a graduate instructor for multiculturalism and education in the preservice teacher education program. Concurrent with her studies, Amina is also a full-time high school English teacher at the Islamic School of Indianapolis, where she teaches logic and rhetoric. She received a Bachelors of Science in neurobiology and physiology at Purdue University with a minor in English and French. Amina is currently doing her master's research on the college experiences of veiling Muslim women who transition from Islamic schools to American campuses. Her research interests include Muslim youth identity in the West, multicultural education, the veil, Islamophobia, and Islamic schools as alternative schooling spaces.

Lyubov Sylayeva completed an MSEd in literacy and language education in the Department of Curriculum and Instruction at Purdue University. Prior to coming to Purdue, she completed a Master of Library and Information Science at the Kharkov State Institute of Social Studies in the Ukraine, where she also worked as a senior librarian in the College of Communication. Lyubov was born in Moscow, Russia, and moved to the Ukraine after high school.

Jason Ware is a PhD student in curriculum studies in the Department of Curriculum and Instruction at Purdue University. His research interests include, but are not limited to, exploring the ways in which the curriculum of home and community inform Black male consciousness and the implications for non-Black school educators, exploring the ways in which Black students engage with critical pedagogies in classrooms, the unifying effects of critical race theory as a social movement between Black academics and urban communities, autobiography, and psychoanalysis. Jason teaches a multiculturalism in education course to preservice teachers and is part of a research team exploring the impact of study abroad on preservice teachers' understanding of race, gender, and class issues within international contexts.

CPSIA information can be obtained at www.ICGtesting.com
Printed in the USA
LVOW07s1949290315

432450LV00013B/147/P